Jump ... And Your Life Will Appear

An Inch-by-Inch Guide To Making A Major Change

Nancy Levin

HAY HOUSE, INC.

Carlsbad, California • New York City
London • Sydney • Johannesburg
Vancouver • Hong Kong • New Delhi

Published and distributed in the United States by: Hay House, Inc.: www.hay house.com® • *Published and distributed in Australia by:* Hay House Australia Pty. Ltd.: www.hayhouse.com.au • *Published and distributed in the United Kingdom by:* Hay House UK, Ltd.: www.hayhouse.co.uk • *Published and distributed in the Republic of South Africa by:* Hay House SA (Pty), Ltd.: www .hayhouse.co.za • *Distributed in Canada by:* Raincoast Books: www.raincoast .com • *Published in India by:* Hay House Publishers India: www.hayhouse.co.in

Cover design: Michelle Polizzi

Originally published by Balboa Press (ISBN 978-1-4525-8857-5).

Cataloging-in-Publication Data is on file at the Library of Congress

Tradepaper ISBN: 978-1-4019-4712-5

17 16 15 14   4 3 2 1
1st Hay House edition, 2014

Printed in the United States of America

SUSTAINABLE FORESTRY INITIATIVE
Certified Chain of Custody
Promoting Sustainable Forestry
www.sfiprogram.org
SFI-01268

SFI label applies to the text stock

"It was an honor to be a firsthand witness to Nancy on her journey through telling the truth, letting go of the past, and making transformational changes in her world. Take her advice, and you too can create a whole new life for yourself."

—Louise Hay, *New York Times* bestselling author of *You Can Heal Your Life*

"Nancy Levin is one powerful woman, trust me. I urge you to read this book and grow."

—Dr. Wayne W. Dyer, *New York Times* bestselling author of *I Can See Clearly Now*

"*Jump … And Your Life Will Appear* teaches us that dark nights of the soul can transform into our brightest awakening. Rebirth is possible, and Nancy Levin's candid story and coaching techniques will show you how. This book is brave, authentic, and liberating. It's filled with spiritual medicine and hope. If there's a truth you've been denying—jump and read this book. Don't waste one more second on autopilot. Your life needs you."

—Kris Carr, *New York Times* bestselling author of *Crazy Sexy Kitchen*

"*Jump … And Your Life Will Appear* is full of the medicine of truth, the heart and writing of a poet, and the torch of light that illuminates the path to wholeness and freedom for others. I loved it."

—Christiane Northrup, MD, *New York Times* bestselling author of *Women's Bodies, Women's Wisdom*, and *The Wisdom of Menopause*

"Truly, this book is a jewel, a genuine gift of heart felt wisdom that should be read by every person who has or is experiencing an emotional life change."
—Caroline Myss, *New York Times* bestselling author of *Sacred Contracts* and *Defy Gravity*

"Jump … And Your Life Will Appear is a must-read for anyone experiencing or considering a major life change. Nancy Levin has written a magnificently relatable, soul-baring, and honest book about how it feels to take a leap of faith . . . and grow stronger and wiser because of this decision. Nancy and her book will coach you each step of the way!"
—Doreen Virtue, bestselling author of *Assertiveness for Earth Angels*

"Jump … And Your Life Will Appear is the perfect guidebook for anyone ready to step into their highest potential. Nancy Levin will help you stop hiding, face your fears, and access the courage to live the life you've been waiting for. With the support of this book you can create radical change."
—Gabrielle Bernstein, *New York Times* bestselling author of *May Cause Miracles*

"Wow! What a compelling, beautiful and much needed book. We all face change in our lives, but many of us are afraid to make the real changes we need to. This book is the perfect guide to transforming your life, as Nancy says, "inch by inch". A must read!"
—Nick Ortner, *New York Times* bestselling author of *The Tapping Solution*

"With immense amount of grit, honesty and determined prose Nancy Levin takes readers towards their own undeniable truth about their lives. Once there she helps them take the leap they should have taken years ago. And she does it masterfully, inch by inch and step by step. *Jump … And Your Life Will Appear* will make you feel as if your best friend walked into your house and not only witnessed your truth but helped you remove the mask you have been holding on to for so long."

—Christina Rasmussen, author of *Second Firsts: Live, Laugh and Love Again*

Contents

Introduction
My Own Jump ... Inch by Inch

I was at the San Diego airport, waiting to board my plane home after having produced Hay House's first "I Can Do It At Sea" cruise. It was April 12, 2008—one of those dates in my life that I'll never forget, the kind that lives in infamy forever.

I looked at my phone and noticed a voicemail that came in while I was going through security. As I listened, the tone of my husband's voice literally made my knees buckle. The next thing I knew, I was collapsed on the carpet at the gate while everyone else began boarding the plane around me. My body was both burning and frozen as I listened to this man who had been my husband for nearly eighteen years. The tone of his voice was crushing, and the words were pure threat.

"I read your journals. You'd better get your ass home—there's hell to pay."

All I could think was that I had more than seventy journals. Which parts had he read?

To this day, I have no recollection of getting on the plane or flying or even listening to the multiple voicemails he left for me while I was in the air. I didn't answer his calls while I was in the car on my way home from the airport.

I felt like I was in an earthquake. Only instead of the ground, it was the life I had built that was crumbling beneath my feet.

After the plane landed in Denver, I drove straight to Boulder, where I live. But I didn't go home. Instead, I went to the St. Julien Hotel, got a room, and left my bags there. Then I walked the two blocks to my apartment—and my husband. I was in a daze, but I can still vividly remember what it was like to stand at the base of the stairs, my heart pounding out of my chest, wondering how I was going to make it up the three flights to my front door.

He'd heard me coming and was waiting just inside the door. He held up four of my journals and announced that he was going to make copies of certain pages and send them to my parents, my sister, my friends, and my coworkers. He looked forward to seeing what they thought of me, once they knew the *real* me.

The sting in my mouth was the bitter taste of a marriage crashing.

The truth is that our relationship had been slowly falling apart for quite some time. I'd chosen to stay in denial so deeply that it had taken something this monumental to wake me up. Suddenly, I had a choice: I could stay numb and go back to sleep, or I could face my fears and embrace change.

I could stand still, or I could get ready for the greatest jump of my life.

*　　*　　*

hourglass: a last love poem

written on the morning I finally filed for divorce

i loved you
as much as i could
as long as i could
hard as i could
hard as it was

steadily holding on
to the small piece of maybe
that was finally destroyed

i have done all i can

we came together
in our respective corners
at the bottom of an hourglass
with our own strengths
our own wounds

marriage is to be found
in the voyage
through the tiny neck
of this timepiece

crossing up and over
to the opposite quadrants
those qualities of the other
missing in ourselves
are to be absorbed
for each to become whole

my love
hard as we tried
we simply did not make it
through the passage

the wounds too deep
the rage too loud
the voice too silent

and though i love you
i cannot be
married to you
i lost myself
in the giving of everything
to you

i now know
heartbreak in one
is a pain
unable to be healed
by the other

we can only
heal ourselves

for months
i have been nowhere
and everywhere
wheeling my home behind me
into the havens of others
now i need to land safely
inside the space of my own

i was starving to death
before hunger finally saved my life
waking me to desire

and now you are free
from the wanting more
than i could give
and i will love you
beyond the wound

*   *   *

Making the Jump

It was a little over two years from the fateful day my husband read my journals to the day I finally made that jump and filed for divorce. Leaving my marriage was the hardest thing I have ever done. It was as if I was jumping off a cliff in hopes of saving my life, without really knowing what—if anything—would catch me.

But somehow, the ground appeared beneath my feet as I landed. And what's more, the most miraculous things began to occur. Doors opened. Unforeseen opportunities presented themselves. I not only survived, I have thrived.

It wasn't always pretty, and it wasn't always easy. But it was so deeply worth it.

That two-year period prior to the jump was filled with pain, fear, and wonderful growth—learning that gave birth to the transformative process I'm offering you in this book.

As the Event Director for Hay House, I've been lucky enough to have traveled for more than a decade with some of the greatest minds of our time in the fields of self-help, inspiration, motivation and wellness. When my marriage came crashing down, I relied on their teachings to make it through. A couple of them even used me as a spiritual guinea pig, trying out self-empowerment experiments on me. All their attention, love, and wisdom eventually led me to undertake my own journey toward helping others. I immersed myself in my dear friend and mentor Debbie Ford's shadow work and eventually became a Certified Integrative Coach. I wrote my first book, *Writing for My Life*—a compilation of poetry, a kind of poetic memoir—as I was leaving my marriage and finding my own voice.

I started speaking at the Hay House "I Can Do It!" conferences, which has led to many more speaking engagements and opportunities. And I was even able to open my heart and fall in love again.

But all of those changes are simply outward signs of a transformation that happened inside of me. Since my divorce, I have become—thankfully—more myself than I ever thought I could be. I have learned who I am when I'm living life for *me*. I've become familiar with the stranger I had been living with for forty-five years: the real Nancy Levin—the woman I'd always been underneath the masks I had been wearing for so long.

And you know what? I really, really like her.

This book is the culmination of all of those experiences. It's my story, and the chronicle of what I have learned along the way. While I lived it, I "felt my way" through the process, but later, specific steps that I had taken began to emerge in my consciousness. It became clear through working with my clients in my coaching practice that I had a powerful roadmap others could follow if they adapted my route to their own circumstances. That's how *Jump … And Your Life Will Appear* was born.

An Inch-by-Inch Guide

What about you? Are you hiding in your life? Have you been called to make changes that you've been too afraid to make? If so, this book is meant to give you the courage and faith you need to feel supported as you jump into your new and better life. It's an "inch-by-inch" guide to help you, the reader, clear the path ahead and move toward letting go and leaping.

I will walk you through a step-by-step process that will take you beyond the fear of jumping … to the moment you jump … to the adjustments that come after you jump. Each step is geared toward helping you make a thorough shift that will improve the quality of your life on all levels.

This book is highly interactive, so what you put into it is what you will get out of it. The exercises at the end of each step will require some deep work on your part, but the rewards are well worth it. Otherwise the reading will just stay in the intellectual realm, and that isn't where healing takes place. Healing will only come from looking within yourself and getting to know your essence—the truth and heart of who you are deep inside. As you work through the exercises, remember that the commitment you make is to yourself and the life you deserve.

The steps are also geared toward giving you a softer place to land as you move forward one inch at a time … and especially after you finally make that all-important jump.

Here's the process we will walk through together:

Step 1: Admit to yourself what you already know. This first step involves some truth-telling. The result is enormously freeing, and it is the primary stepping-stone to *true* freedom.

Step 2: Tell the truth to someone safe. After your admission to yourself, it will be time to trust someone else with your truth.

Step 3: Imagine yourself free. In this step, you will set the stage for freedom by first making it real in your imagination.

Step 4: Make one different choice. Starting small as you work toward your jump (I did say "inch-by-inch"), you will do one thing differently. The results from this one small change may surprise you.

Step 5: Set your new boundaries. You will begin to set solid boundaries where you have allowed them to be violated in the past. Don't worry—you'll be ready for this step by the time you get there.

Step 6: Ask for help. During this step, you'll learn that it's actually wonderful for both parties when you allow yourself to receive.

Step 7: Honor your resistance. As you get primed for your jump, we'll deal together with the inevitable resistance that will tell you that you cannot, must not, and will not jump. Fear not! You *will*.

Step 8: Jump! By the time you've moved through the steps one inch at a time, you'll be ready to make your jump. This step will help you land on softer clouds.

Step 9: The Graceful Exit. Too often, books stop at the point when you're asked to change, not helping you deal with the aftermath. Once you have jumped, there will still be resistance, adjustment, and integration. This step will help you make a smoother transition.

Step 10: Say Yes … And Then Say It Again … And Again. The final step is all about living your new, best life after the jump.

At the end of each step, you will also find "A Moment of Forgiveness." I believe that transformation isn't possible without forgiveness, both of yourself and others. When you don't forgive, a big part of you stays focused on negative, judgmental energy that could be used more productively in your life. As author and teacher Iyanla Vanzant said in her book, *Forgiveness: 21 Days to Forgive Everyone for Everything*, "Forgiveness helps to transform and eliminate the energy blockages that we hold in our minds about who we are and who others are, and the subsequent issues or upsets that grow from the thoughts, beliefs, and judgments we hold." It's an important part of each step, so I urge you to take it to heart!

This Process is Tried and True

I share the story of my process—my "jump"—with you in hopes that some of what you read here will resonate in your own life. Perhaps my story is not just "my" story, but is part of "our" story—the human journey toward finding our true selves and our unique places in this world.

How do I know these steps work? I'm living proof! And so are the clients I coach. In my case, of course, the jump involved a divorce, but for my clients it has worked with any kind of change—whether you want to switch jobs or careers, move to a different part of the world, set boundaries with someone in your life (no matter who it is), do something new that you've hesitated to try, increase your capacity for self-love, or simply move out of fear into profound courage and love. Whatever you want to change, wherever you want to jump, this book is here to support you.

I will continue to share my own story throughout the book, as well as the stories of others, and show how we used each step to move closer to the jumps we would ultimately make. (Note that most names have been changed to protect confidentiality.) I hope you will find comfort and guidance in reading how each of us has put this process into practice.

And remember, this is not a race! It's an *inch-by-inch* guide. Jumping doesn't always require a running start. Your move toward the jump can be a dance. So read the steps at your own pace. Some steps might require more time than others.

My desire is for my words and experience to impact you in exactly the way *you* need. My wish is to benefit all of life—yours, mine, and ours.

Do You Need to Write Down the Exercises?

You don't have to write down all of the answers to the exercises in this book, but I urge you to do so when it's appropriate. There is something about writing it down that makes it more tangible, and you're more likely to remember it if you write it down.

Writing also gives you the opportunity to do something ritualistic with the paper you've written on, which may be meaningful to you at some point—burning it or ripping it into shreds, for example.

If, however, you fear that someone else might find what you've written before you're ready to disclose your secrets, I certainly understand. After my husband found my journals, I destroyed all of them—over seventy volumes. I had been keeping journals since I was eleven years old, and after I felt exposed, I didn't write another journal entry for two years.

If you're concerned about exposure, write down your answers, and rip them up or delete them immediately. You can also do what I did for a while—keep everything saved only on a thumb drive, and carry it around with you everywhere. Or you can keep it all under lock and key. Do what you need to do, but commit the physical act of writing it down—preferably on paper. It does make a difference.

Are you ready? If not, don't worry—we're never really ready. Remember that the process is inch-by-inch, so you can take as much time as you need. (It took me two years to really make the leap of my lifetime.) But let's take a deep breath and dive into the book, at the very least. Because, as I proved with my own journey, you never know what you're going to find on the very next page. Hold tight! This book may look small, but it's action-packed.

Step One
Admit to Yourself What
You Already Know

Within twenty-four hours of moving from New York City to Boulder, Colorado, I met the man who would become my husband. He was tall, gorgeous, charming, and sweet, and he swept me off my feet with a sense of adventure. Three days later, he spent the night … and he never left. (I was the one who finally left, more than eighteen years later).

Before I knew it, I was doing things with this man that I had never done before—camping, skiing, rock climbing, mountain biking, and running marathons. I had thought I would return to New York after finishing my graduate program in poetry in Colorado, but it soon became clear that this city girl was *not* returning to the city.

My husband couldn't have been more wrong for me "on paper." Let's just say he was far from the nice Jewish boy from a good East Coast family I was "supposed" to marry. My family and friends were confused. Why would Nancy choose love the hard way? But the pull was too great. My husband embodied most of the qualities that I had rejected in myself. He valued play, fun, leisure, rest, and adventure over work. For the most part, I classified fun and leisure as irresponsible and lazy. And the clincher was that underneath his masculine bravado, the unspoken whisper from his psyche was, "Hi, I'm broken."

My unspoken whisper in response? "Great! I'm Superwoman. I will fix you."

Our core wounds were a match made in heaven.

My Superwoman complex started when I was two years old. That year, my six-year-old brother died. Severely mentally disabled from birth, he had lived his life utterly incapacitated—broken—until he caught pneumonia, and his immune system could no longer fight. I'm told that even as a small child, I took great pride in my independence. I think I somehow sensed that my parents had their hands full. They were lost in grief, so I learned to take care of myself.

Several beliefs became imprinted within me during that time:

- My wants and needs are insignificant, and no one will be able to meet them anyway.
- I must be perfect in order to make up for my parents' loss and grief.
- Since I'm the one who survived, I am undeserving of joy, yet at the same time, responsible for the happiness of my parents and other people.
- Maybe if I'm perfect and indispensable, then I can fix everything, all will be okay, and I will be loved.
- And the kicker: If I am imperfect—like my poor, sweet brother—I will be disposable and die.

Thus began the quest to become Superwoman from Perfectionville.

These beliefs, of course, were not formed consciously. As a two-year-old, I was hardly aware that I felt the need to be perfect in order to feel safe. Attempting to be perfect was simply an unconscious survival strategy. Like all children, I was trying to figure out who I needed to be and what I needed to do to get the most love possible, while avoiding trouble and pain as much as I could.

Our childhood beliefs may be illogical, but they take hold and become the way we see the world. They are unconscious "shadow beliefs" that become part of our personal operating systems. They tell us what we can and cannot do. The people and situations we attract into our lives are consistent with those beliefs—for better or worse.

As adults, we continue this unconscious, habitual, compulsive way of being without any awareness as to why. It's only when we bring our shadow beliefs into conscious awareness in adulthood that we can see the hold they've had over us as well as the gifts they offer. Then, we can shine light on these unwanted parts of ourselves, stop pushing them away, and integrate them in order to reclaim wholeness. Author and teacher Iyanla Vanzant says, "A belief is a thought—fueled by a feeling—that you think over and over again until it becomes habitual. Once a thought becomes habitual, you no longer even recognize that you are thinking it. For this reason, it is absolutely essential to identify and release the long-held, worn-out beliefs that often hold toxic thoughts in place."

Unfortunately, when I married my husband, I had not yet reached that level of awareness.

What Was in the Journals?

Once my mother knew that my marriage was falling

Nancy Levin

apart, she finally said to me what she had known for a while: "You lost yourself." It was true. My childhood circumstances had turned me into someone with an extreme ability for empathy and endurance. As a result, I did everything for my husband. It was all about him, and my own needs didn't matter.

I had designed a marriage for myself where there was no room for the real me. I acted the part of the woman my husband wanted and needed me to be. But I wasn't good enough, not even at that. So I let him try and mold me into his image of the perfect wife. When he became demanding or controlling, I put my needs aside and tried to be even more of what he wanted.

What happens when you stay in a situation that isn't working, denying your own needs long enough? Your needs, your health, and your well-being begin to demand to be heard. Even if you don't heed that call, the truth will come out. Unfortunately, it will come out sideways. Perhaps you'll become ill. Or depressed. Or if you're like me, you'll find yourself expressing those needs in destructive ways.

What my husband discovered when he read my journals was how my true self had expressed herself sideways. What he read was that eight years earlier, I had an affair.

Looking back, I see that I'd been able to be myself with this other man. I'd been able to be who I *really* am. I didn't need to play the role of the perfect wife. I didn't have to manage my actions and reactions around him. That man loved the real me.

It's still hard for me to disclose that I had an affair. I wish I'd never been that person, and my lifelong preference for perfection lingers. But in a book that is about learning to tell the truth to yourself and others so

4

that you can live your authentic life, I knew I had to tell you—the reader—the truth. So, I am laying myself bare here, mistakes and all.

I'm not proud of what I did. But at the same time, on some level, I understand my own actions as an attempt to connect with my authenticity. A misguided effort, yes, but it was an attempt at finding and becoming my real, essential self.

The woman I am today would have walked away from that marriage rather than have an affair. But as they say, hindsight is 20/20.

Instead, I betrayed my husband. But prior to that, I had betrayed myself. It was self-abandonment that led to my infidelity. I betrayed myself by pretending to be someone I was not. I betrayed myself in my marriage for eighteen years. And that marriage was a long time to be away from me.

Together, my husband and I had managed to build a strong façade for the outside world. I thought everyone must look at our marriage and assume it was picture-perfect, which was just how I wanted it. If I'd walked away, I would've had to admit that the image was false. Because of my deep fear of being imperfect—of being dispensable, like my brother had been—I could not even admit to myself that our marriage wasn't working, let alone admit it to my husband or anyone else.

There was shame for me in admitting that I couldn't live up to my own idea of who I thought I "should" be. And my idea, of course, was impossible: the perfect Superwoman who could fix anything and juggle everything, without ever letting a ball drop. None of us are capable of that, no matter how hard we try.

As author and teacher Brené Brown says, "Perfectionism is a shield that we carry with a thought process that says, 'If I look perfect, live perfect, work perfect, and do it all perfectly, I can avoid or minimize feeling shame, blame, and judgment.'" She's so right.

Still, underneath the façade of perfection, somewhere deep down where I dared not look, I knew my marriage wasn't working. I knew for a long time that I wasn't really happy. But it took me years to admit to myself what I already knew.

A big hope I have for this book is that, by sharing my own experience, I might spare you what I went through. With that in mind, I ask you this: What are you afraid to tell yourself that somewhere deep down you already know?

Admitting What You Already Know

When something is "off" in your life, you know it. And it takes an incredible amount of energy to continue the denial—energy that could be used toward letting go of the old and inviting in the new. That's what I learned when things finally fell apart. The new was so much better. If I had just been able to let go sooner, I could have started that new life years before.

What about you? What have you not yet admitted to yourself that you already know? If you aren't happy with your life, or with some specific aspect of your life, there is probably something you haven't been willing to tell yourself.

Revealing Questions

1. Asking yourself a series of questions can sometimes help you unearth information from deep within. Below are some key questions that are geared toward bringing to the surface what you already know but have not admitted to yourself:

   - What would you not want to tell your best friend?
   - What inside of you would you hide if you had a camera crew in your house shooting a reality show? (And I mean serious things *within you*, not silly physical stuff like the dust bunnies under the couch or the donuts in the cupboard. For example, it might be something as serious as an eating disorder or as commonplace as wanting to quit your job.)
   - What do you feel shame about?
   - What do you feel you must hide in order for people to love you?

2. Write about something you absolutely cannot write about. You might even want to begin by writing these words on the page: "I absolutely cannot write about…"

3. Write a poem if that's easier for you. Poet David Whyte says, "Poetry is often the art of overhearing yourself say things you didn't know you knew. It is a learned skill to force yourself to articulate your life, your present world or your possibilities for the future. We need that same

skill as an art of survival. We need to overhear the tiny but very consequential things we say that reveal ourselves to ourselves." You might start the poem with "I'm overhearing myself say…"

A while Back for me it was living at M at!

4. What in your life is not working? Ask yourself additional questions about your life and relationships:

- How well are your relationships working—significant other, parents, siblings, children, relatives, friends, coworkers, bosses?
- How well are your career and finances working?
- Are you taking care of your health, both physical and spiritual?
- What isn't working in your life, and what do *Plenty* you already know about why it isn't working?
- What have you not told yourself yet about why it isn't working? *In the past now*

The Easy Way Out?

When we betray ourselves and others, it's often because we've made the easier choice—consciously or unconsciously. This so-called easier choice is almost always the cowardly choice. For example, I mistakenly believed that it was easier for me to have an affair than to tell myself and my husband the truth. As is usually the case in situations like these, I was wrong.

Eventually, making the cowardly choice will be harder, not easier at all, because it will almost inevitably lead to destruction. You may be delaying the "blow out," but once it comes, that blow out is often bigger and more painful the longer you put it off. I'm certain the pain would have been less and my self-esteem would have remained intact had I been in alignment with myself and with my husband.

But we're all human, and we've all taken the "easy" way out at some point in our lives.

What about you? Are you doing anything now that is the easy thing, as opposed to the honest thing? What are you doing in your life that is self-sabotaging?

In 2015 nothing I think

Natalia Tells Her Story

The day I said no to my bulimia was liberating and life-changing. It was the hardest thing I'd ever done. I had come to be comforted by this strange addiction of binging … zoning out until I felt sick, and then the purging, washing it all away, forgetting it ever happened. Relief. A clean slate. It was so cyclical and became a part of my everyday life. It controlled me. I would stand up, wipe away the tears in the mirror (my face flushed and puffy), brush my beautiful, long, brown hair back, and force a weak smile.

The day I finally admitted what I already knew, I lay on my bed and cried so hard that my stomach muscles burned. I curled into a ball and wept like a broken little girl who was somehow growing into a woman. I cried for so many things—so many moments that had affected and shaped me. I was a four-year-old crying for her parents to stop fighting. I was a ten-year-old wishing her Dad wouldn't drink anymore. I was a fifteen-year-old second-guessing her beautiful slender

---

athletic body. I was a seventeen-year-old navigating the untreaded waters of freedom.

I was twenty the day I married myself and left the past behind. I made my vows: "...to have and to hold from this day forward, for better, for worse, for richer, for poorer, in sickness and health, until death do us part." I promised to love and cherish myself forever. I went to the mall and stopped at a small ring stand, slipping a perfectly simple sterling silver ring onto my right ring finger, and it has since resided there. It's a beautiful reminder of the vows that I've held since that time in my life.

I am twenty-seven now, and although I am healthy and happy, I still catch myself lifting my shirt in the mirror, turning sideways to try and find the imperfections. Deep down, I know there are none. About a year ago, while in the grocery store, I put a pack of butter in my basket and felt a few tears streaming down my face. I was crying because for the first time in my life, I had no guilt.

I know it sounds silly. I have everything and I am everything. It has been a process to get to where I am now. You would look at me today and say, "She is so pretty and athletic and smart." And it's because I am, and I know it and cherish it.

What Are You Committed To?

For eighteen years, I thought I was committed to my marriage. But in hindsight, I realize I was actually committed to being indispensable. That led me to stay in an unhappy marriage even if it was a lie. That commitment overrode my desire for my own well-being and happiness.

What I've learned is that, in life, we get what we're committed to at the deepest level. We tell ourselves we're committed to happiness, but deep down, we're actually committed to something else—like being indispensable, staying safe, or putting others' needs ahead of our own. Generally these commitments are based on shadow beliefs developed in childhood.

For example, many of us are committed to being punished in some way. Some tenacious childhood belief keeps us thinking we deserve punishment. In her book, *The Right Questions*, my dear friend and mentor Debbie Ford said, "Our outer world reflects our inner commitments. If we want to know what we are really committed to, all we have to do is look at our lives. We are, whether we are aware of it or not, always creating exactly what we are most committed to. It is vital to understand that the choices we make are always in alignment with our deepest commitments. By examining what we have and what we don't have, we will be able to uncover and see what we are truly committed to. When our lives are not the way we want them to be, we can be certain we have a conflicting hidden—underlying—commitment to something other than that which we say we are committed to."

Check Your Commitments

1. What do you get in life repeatedly that you don't want? not much

2. What might you be unconsciously committed to, which keeps bringing these unwanted circumstances into your life? *I just Have a hard time finding an extra job*

Who Are You Really?

Author Beryl Markham said, "You can live a lifetime and, at the end of it, know more about other people than you know about yourself." Louise Hay told me that I deserved an Academy Award for my portrayal as the "perfect wife." What roles do you play, and how well do you know your authentic self?

In this exercise, you will create four descriptions of yourself based on the roles you play in life. *It's especially important to write these down so that you can compare them when you're finished.* Be thorough with each description, and take the time to really think about your answers.

1. How would acquaintances and coworkers in your world describe you? Write your description as a list of characteristics or as a narrative of how they see you.

2. How would your immediate family describe you? How do your spouse and children see you? How do your parents and siblings see you? If your spouse, children, parents, and/or siblings see you in different ways, write more than one description.

3. Who do you tell yourself you are? How would *you* describe yourself?

4. Who are you afraid to tell yourself you are? Here's an example for you: When my marriage started to crumble, my therapist referred to me as an "adulteress." I said, "No, I'm not that!" She said, "Yes, you are." And she was right, of course. I just didn't want to admit to myself that I had become something I never wanted to be. I didn't see myself as an adulteress, but my behavior said otherwise.

    For this particular description, however, watch for the tendency to beat yourself up. We deceive ourselves in all sorts of ways. While I didn't want to admit something negative about myself, I also didn't want to fall into the trap of judging myself too harshly. For example, you might tell yourself that you aren't good enough simply because you expect yourself to be perfect. That isn't fair, either.

5. Place all of your character descriptions side by side, and review them carefully. How different are they? Where are there disconnects from one to the other? Is there, for example, a big gap between #1 (the way the world describes you) and #4 (the you that you're afraid to tell yourself you are)? If you are out of alignment, the goal is to begin to become the real you in all areas of your life.

Creating Alignment

For so long, my self-worth was tied up in how much

of a chameleon I could be. How much could I please people? How well could I turn myself into what they needed? Becoming what they wanted brought me the most validation, but it was a false validation. I was loved for my façade, not for me. When I finally let the façade go, I discovered that, yes, there were people in the world who would love me for my true self, even though I wasn't perfect. I learned that I could not only survive if I was human, but actually thrive because of it.

We are meant to be fully and truly who we are. If we're living authentically, we might show different aspects of our personalities in different situations, *but none of them will be false.*

It's impossible to maintain a false identity without consequences. It takes a lot of energy to hold up a mask, to continue a story, to portray a role that isn't true. When you stop and tell the truth, so much energy becomes available to you—energy that can be used to live the life you want.

Do your character descriptions in the previous exercise reveal that you have been living out of alignment with your true self? What masks do you wear in your life? How true to yourself are you in *all* areas of your life? Is the person you have been in your life authentic to who you are, or is it a composite of the tricks you've learned in order to navigate your life—like driving around potholes in an effort to dodge possible landmines?

What Would It Be Like to Live Authentically?

What would happen if all of your character descriptions were in alignment? Imagine what would be available to you—energy, time, insight, freedom, fun, etc.—if you let the mask fall and committed to just being you. What would it be like to be that transparent, genuine, and organic in your life? Can you imagine it? Remember what visionary poet William Blake said: "What is now proved was once only imagined."

Write down your vision, or make a collage that shows what it would be like.

Whose Life Are You Living?

For years, I sublimated my own desires in service of my husband's. I wasn't living my own life.

Poet David Whyte has said that if you are living the life you are meant to live, someone will inevitably feel betrayed by it. My ex-husband can legitimately say that I betrayed him by having an affair. But would I also have betrayed him if I had become my true self in our marriage? He might have felt so. It would have meant putting myself and my own needs before his, but that's what I was too scared to do. Since then, I have learned that betraying yourself can never be the price you pay to avoid betraying someone else. We don't serve anyone if we are pretending. We only serve *their* façade—the part of them that is in denial and unwilling to admit what *they* already know. We don't owe anyone the denial of who we are.

Make Room for a New Story

Debbie Ford wrote, "We cannot accept a situation until we're ready to look fearlessly at the facts of our circumstances. Acceptance comes when we step out of denial and judgment and are willing to see the present exactly as it exists in this moment, without any drama or story line. Drama keeps us stuck in an endless spiral of excuses that prevent us from being able to distinguish between fact and fantasy. Our drama serves as a defense mechanism designed to protect us from the pain of our past. When we're caught up in our drama, we are no longer living in the present moment. Instead, we get hooked into every similar experience from our past that was left unhealed. We think we are responding to the challenges of our lives when in fact we are reacting to all of our unresolved pain."

So, most of the pain we create in our lives is due to stories we tell ourselves that aren't true—the inability to separate fact from fiction. Why do we choose to tell ourselves false stories? Because we don't want to face "what is." Reality feels threatening to us, but reality has a way of forcing us to accept it eventually. The truth won't be denied forever, as I can attest.

What Stories Do You Tell Yourself?

1. "A story I tell myself is _____, but the truth is _____.

   "A story I tell myself is _____, but the truth is _____.

   "A story I tell myself is _____, but the truth is _____.

2. If writing it down becomes difficult for you, try making a collage of the story you tell yourself, followed by a collage of the true story. Allow yourself to choose images that "feel" right even if you aren't sure why. How are the collages different? What can you learn about yourself from the images?

3. Set a timer, and sit in front of a mirror for three minutes. Admit to yourself out loud where in your life you're held back, dissatisfied, unhappy, or blocked. What do you already know about these circumstances?

Go Gently Down the Stream...

If you've done all of the exercises in this step, you may have opened up some very difficult truths. If that's the case, breathe in ... exhale ... breathe in again ... and exhale.

This is not the end of the process—it's only the beginning. Stick with me, and I'll take your hand as we walk gently, step-by-step, to the moment when you can make a real positive change in your life. (Of course, if you feel compelled to do so as a result of what you have unearthed, by all means, seek professional therapeutic support. Take care of you!)

The jump that I'm encouraging you to make through the process of this book is about facing what is true. It's only through facing the truth that you will be able to fulfill your potential and live the life you were meant to live. It's only by jumping that you will be able to fly.

A MOMENT TO FORGIVE

While it took a long time, I had to eventually forgive myself for my infidelity. I had to forgive myself for not being in integrity. By the same token, I had to forgive my ex-husband for his controlling nature, and for wanting me to be the woman he wanted rather than the woman I was.

Take a moment, right now, to affirm that you will forgive yourself for whatever you need to forgive—including the stories you have told yourself that are not true. We all tell ourselves false stories. We're human. But now is the time to forgive yourself and make a new commitment to truth and the joy it can bring.

Step Two
Tell the Truth to Someone Safe

Up until that day I found out my husband had read my journals, I had never told anyone about my affair. I mean nobody—not my dear sister, not my closest friends, no one. Looking back, I can hardly believe I kept it to myself that long! Today, I would *have* to tell *somebody*. But I'd compartmentalized my life to such a degree that it wasn't even hard to keep it a secret. I was afraid of the shame; paralyzed at the thought of what people would think of me. My motto had long been "Never let them see you sweat," and I wasn't about to reveal myself.

My husband, of course, knew just which buttons to push. His greatest threat after he read the journals was exposure. He was going to pin the scarlet letter on me himself, telling my friends and family what I had done. Naturally I was terrified. I'd spent so long believing that I wouldn't get love if I were imperfect, that I assumed everyone would turn away from me if they found out. I assumed I'd be left alone.

Eight years had passed since my infidelity, but the truth suddenly felt like a weight I could no longer bear by myself. So before I even faced my husband—on my drive home from the airport that fateful day—I did something that was very difficult for me. In spite of my motto, *I told the truth to someone safe.*

I called my dear friend, Cheryl Richardson, from the car and spilled everything. After listening to the whole story, she said, "I don't think you should stay at home tonight. If you decide to go talk to him, make sure you have an exit strategy and somewhere to go." She hadn't hung up on me or told me I was a horrible person. Instead she was offering loving support and *advice*!

During that phone call, I could almost feel my perfect façade beginning to crack. Even though I was terrified, the terror was mixed with a distinct feeling of relief. The "story" I had told myself for so many years was coming apart. I didn't know it then, but the moment I let myself be truly seen, I started letting go of the role I had played in the world for so long. By telling Cheryl, I finally allowed myself to be vulnerable. I finally allowed myself to be known as the imperfect human being I am.

In that moment, the mask fell. It felt like a huge weight lifted. Cheryl was a true friend, willing to be a witness to my truth while also holding me accountable for it. And all I knew was that I no longer had to carry the burden of the truth alone.

Imperfections are not inadequacies; they are
reminders that we're all in this together.
—Brené Brown

In the first step, you admitted to yourself what you already knew. The next step in the process is to confide in someone else what you have discovered. I know very well how hard this can be, so choose someone safe— someone who loves you and won't judge you. Take a moment to think about who you might tell. If you can't think of anyone yet, don't worry. As you continue with the next steps, I firmly believe that the right person will come to mind.

The Fear of Vulnerability

Another of Brené Brown's great quotes is: "The first thing we look for in someone else is vulnerability, and the last thing we want to reveal to anyone is our vulnerability." What a paradox! When we allow ourselves to be vulnerable in front of others, they see our humanness. They can have compassion for us on a deep, genuine level. Yet we're so scared! We're afraid others will see us as unworthy or unlovable, so we feel we must hide our vulnerabilities.

While the fear of revealing yourself is natural, doing so unburdens you. It actually helps you *overcome* the fear of judgment. Why? Because we discover that people aren't judging us nearly as harshly as we expect. In fact, in my experience, people *rarely* judge us harshly when we show vulnerability. The biggest issue is how much we judge ourselves.

So often we perceive rejection that isn't there. I once gave a keynote speech at Hay House's "I Can Do It! Ignite NYC" conference. There, in front of 2,500 people, I had shared my story of being a "recovering perfectionist." I explained how, historically, I've felt self-worth only based on external validation. Now one of my roles as the Event Director at Hay House is to stand backstage with the presenters. I give each one a little pep talk on their way onstage and greet each one with a squeeze and some words of praise when they're done.

I had neglected to assign anyone the duty of playing that role for *me* after I finished my talk, so no one showered me with compliments the moment I walked off stage. Without a second thought, I defaulted to my habit of negative self-talk. I even began to send texts from backstage to apologize for how poorly I had performed.

Ironic, huh? But, as they say, we teach what we need to learn.

When I emerged a bit later for my book signing, still in a negative fog of my own making, I could barely receive the overwhelmingly positive response that awaited me. I was showered with compliments by audience members and colleagues alike. Moreover, they told me that I ran off stage so quickly that I missed my standing ovation! Wow—what a lesson! So many of the judgments we expect to receive from others turn out to be coming from within.

I'm not saying you'll never get judged or criticized. All of us have revealed vulnerable parts of ourselves to others, only to have them express judgments. But it doesn't mean we need to go into hiding.

Hiding is actually a way of giving up on life. Only by fully participating in life—letting others see us for all of who we are—can we live the full life we all want so much. We can't be loved for all of who we are unless we allow ourselves to be *seen* for all of who we are. If I had not been willing to stand up that day and offer my vulnerability in front of all those people, I wouldn't have experienced such wonderful connections on the other side.

Luckily, you don't have to start your vulnerability journey by giving a talk to 2,500 people or confessing your deepest secrets in a book. Start with one safe person you trust. If you are truly afraid you might be judged, ask the person to try hard to suspend judgment. Then, before you reveal your truth, tell your safe person exactly what you want to hear in response. For example, you could say that all you want to hear as you speak is one or more of these statements:

"I understand."

"I accept you."

"I love you."

"You are safe."

"It's okay."

Melinda Tells Her Story

When I went to Peru, my husband, Frank, and I were already wondering about the direction of our marriage. In part, we went to Peru to get clear if we should stay together or not. For the first week, we had several discussions about this, feeling into it. On the second week of our trip, a dear girlfriend of mine joined the group, and I found out that Frank had arranged and paid for her to come. As days went on, their connection was more apparent and obvious to the group. Frank would sit next to her during meals, and they would gaze into each other's eyes for long periods of time. I felt great responsibility because it seemed that if I said anything, it would disrupt the group too much. So I just held it all in, most of the time feeling suffocated, holding my breath, and with that my tears, my scream of hurt and anguish, and unbearable self-loathing.

One night after dinner, someone else in the group (Doris), asked to walk with me along the boardwalk. She asked me how I was doing. I was very tentative at first, just giving hints of how uncomfortable the experience was. I wasn't saying what I really wanted

---

23

to say until I blurted out, "Is it too much to ask to be special?" I will never forget the tenderness and love I saw in Doris' eyes. It was not so much her answer, which was simply something like, "Of course not!" It was the *love* I felt from her. I felt *seen*, and in that moment, I knew I was not crazy to feel the way I felt. I was not crazy that it hurt so much to be ignored. I was not crazy to want congruence in my relationship with my husband.

So, I went to my room with a new-found strength and resolution in me. I waited for what seemed an eternity for him to come back. When he did, I said, "If I'm going to be your wife, this has to stop. I want you to acknowledge me here and with the group." He said something to the effect that I was so selfish and self-centered, that I didn't understand love, and that he loved everyone equally. To that, I said, "I'm not everyone, I'M YOUR WIFE, and if I'm going to be like everyone, then we are going to behave as such."

What happened next never would have happened had I not shared my deepest pain with Doris. I packed my bags and booked a separate room. I did not leave the group or the program. I stayed! We had yet another week to go! My marriage had ended, and I had to remember how to walk alone. And I did! I stood up for myself and my truth, and I became stronger and stronger on my own two feet.

Cultivating Vulnerability and Trust

If trusting another person feels scary, it helps to begin to heal those times when your trust has been betrayed. We've all had that experience, but we can't live our lives never trusting anyone again because of it. Learning to trust another is actually about learning to trust yourself.

1. Think about the times when your trust has been betrayed—when you have revealed something about yourself and felt judged for it by another. Recognize that each individual's inability to show you compassion came out of their own self-judgment and fear. Affirm that you will forgive each person.

    I forgive _____ for judging me.
    I forgive _____ for judging me.
    I forgive _____ for judging me.

2. Write from the voice of fear and judgment within yourself. I call this my "inner critic crawl." It's sort of like the CNN crawl—that ongoing text at the bottom of the TV screen. What does your "inner critic crawl" say? Give this voice inside you a chance to speak so that you can see how demanding it can be. Here is some of mine: "You should never have betrayed your husband. And why on earth did you write it all down? You were just asking for it, idiot. You should never let anyone see the real you because they're just going to see how imperfect and unacceptable you really are. You'll never be loved, and you'll end up all alone."

    Harsh, right? But by giving this part of you voice, you can see clearly how no one could live up to your inner critic's expectations. Once you've written it down, feel free to delete it, burn it, or rip it to shreds.

3. In the first step, you worked on discovering what you already knew. What are you most afraid will happen if you reveal these secrets to someone? How likely is it that this fear will come true? If you feel it's likely your fear will come true, can you think of someone safer who you can tell?

> If I tell someone the truth, I'm afraid _____.
> If I tell someone the truth, I'm afraid _____.
> If I tell someone the truth, I'm afraid _____.

4. Visualize telling your secret to someone safe. Imagine it in detail. Hear yourself in your mind telling the person your story, and hear the positive responses you receive back. How does it feel in your body to tell your secret?

    Now, feel nothing but love coming from the other person. Recognize that the love you feel is actually the love you're capable of offering yourself. Can you give yourself that love even though you aren't perfect? Can you love yourself if you're imperfect? How does it feel in your body to receive that love? Can you let it in?

5. Think about how and why you have learned to be invulnerable in your life. What are some of the reasons we as human beings try to be invulnerable?

Amy Tells Her Story

I told my coach that I'd had a very brief affair whilst being married. I had been a client of hers for some time, possibly as long as two years. I felt ready to truly face this truth about myself, and I was at a place where I didn't know what to do with the information. I was close to confessing to my husband, but I wanted to be sure I wasn't going to do that just to make myself feel better.

First off, she thanked me for confiding in her. My fear told me she would think differently of me, and maybe be distant or (in my worst fear) let me go as a client. But she didn't. She was ready to help, and didn't once judge me.

She told me to journal, and I relived the whole affair again. I felt it fully, rather than push it from my mind and reality, pretending it didn't really happen.

I got to know myself as the woman who deeply loved her husband, but who also had an affair. I saw the complexity of the situation, and I stopped judging myself so harshly.

Telling her helped me own up to what I had done. Once someone else knew and asked questions, it made it real. I suddenly saw the affair not as a blip on my perfect record, but as a necessary part of my life.

Telling her made me whole.

The big change that came from telling my darkest secret to a loving presence was that I learned to accept myself and the life I want to live. It isn't a conventional life. I am not a conventional woman. I became more of me. I realized I don't have to be the perfect person living the perfect life. I just need to be the truthful me living an authentic life. I learned to be kinder to myself, especially when I do things I am not proud of. (I always had that the wrong way around. I need to be kinder to myself when things are difficult, not harder on myself!)

Admitting my darkest secret to someone else started a whole process of self-acceptance at a deep level. I'm grateful, and I have, at last, forgiven myself.

The Price of Secrets

Three things cannot be long hidden—
the sun, the moon, and the truth.
—Buddhist saying

After letting my secret out, I felt such relief. I discovered how much more energy it was taking to hold onto it than to be transparent and authentic. What does keeping a secret do to us internally?

In an article in the February 2007 issue of *O: The Oprah Magazine,* writer Martha Beck said, "Secrets are like stars. They're hot, volatile concentrations of energy, and they have two ways of dying. Over time, small stars simply burn out and cool off, becoming what astronomers call white dwarfs. Massive stars collapse in on themselves, growing so dense that they create an immense gravitational vortex from which even light can't escape. They become black holes."

These "black holes" at the center of our lives—these masks that we wear—take an enormous amount of energy to maintain. There's a wonderful Chinese proverb that expresses it well: "Tension is who you think you should be. Relaxation is who you are."

Stop and think about it: What is the cost of holding on to the mask versus the cost of letting go? Only you can answer that question, and it's worth looking into. Take the time to think about it seriously, being as honest with yourself as possible. Then, allow yourself to feel the relief of sharing your vulnerability with someone safe.

A MOMENT TO FORGIVE

Earlier in this step, you wrote down the names of people who have judged you and affirmed that you would forgive them. Yet, we tend to judge ourselves more harshly than anyone else does. So, take a moment now to forgive yourself (1) for being an imperfect person, (2) for judging yourself so harshly, (3) for being afraid to share your vulnerabilities with others, and (4) for being afraid to live as fully as you could. That forgiveness is the first step to living the life you truly deserve.

Step Three
Imagine Yourself Free

In the last few months of my marriage, I lived out of a suitcase. My husband had kicked me out of the house for the fifth time, and I was staying with loved ones all across the country as we tried to reconcile. One refuge for me was Cheryl Richardson's house. She has a beautiful round sitting room that looks out at a reservoir, and I spent lots of time with her there, drinking tea and talking for hours. In one particularly memorable conversation, Cheryl said something that hit me hard— like a blow to my belly.

"It's time that you allow yourself to *fantasize* about being divorced."

At that time, I was still trying to repair my marriage, and I was unable to accept that the end was inevitable. The fear mind certainly has a hold over our decision-making! I was so sure I wouldn't survive the end of my marriage that I refused to even consider letting go. Giving any airtime to Cheryl's suggestion seemed like a betrayal of that belief.

I felt threatened and victimized by my husband, yet I felt so guilty for my transgression that I was simultaneously at his mercy. I believed that I deserved to be punished and that I had to do anything he asked, even if I didn't want to do it, in order to make up for what I had done. The affair detonated the bomb of the childhood wounds in each of us, except my husband did not want to look at his wounds and try to heal them.

"You screwed this up," he told me repeatedly, "so you fix it." All of his repressed rage came to the surface, and he became a tyrant. He went so far as to announce that our marriage was no longer a democracy—I had no say anymore.

I had convinced myself that I could stay with him and still get all of my needs met, but it just wasn't possible. Eventually, it became clear that "making up for it" would never end. By staying in my marriage, I wasn't allowing the full expression of my life to emerge, and looking back, I realize that the marriage was another hiding place for me. As long as I stayed and propped him up, I could hide from what I truly wanted and from all I was capable of becoming. Leaving my husband meant I would no longer have excuses for not fully inhabiting my life—a terrifying thought.

As Brené Brown says, "Momentary discomfort is better than long-term resentment." So much of the time, we would rather stay small and imprisoned than face the uncertainty of becoming who we are meant to be. The resentment that comes with keeping our dreams under wraps may be a life sentence, but it's also a known commodity. It's within our comfort zone. In order to stay there, we have to slip into denial, numb out, and stuff down our real feelings and our true selves. What a high cost we pay for that so-called "comfort."

I became aware that my denial had caused an underlying tension in almost everything I did, and tension is the opposite of freedom. In my career, people-pleasing and workaholism became escapes. I kept jumping through hoop after hoop in order to receive recognition and earn a gold star. But no amount of gold stars was ever enough to fill the emptiness of living an inauthentic life.

235595

My hard work was also an attempt to be good and "do things right." In my mind, being wrong meant I'd be punished—which, on a deep level, is what I expected most of the time. In her book, *The Right Questions,* Debbie Ford asks, "Am I looking for what is right, or am I looking for what is wrong?" I was always, always looking for what I was doing wrong.

That truth was brought home to me one day when I went grocery shopping with Cheryl's husband, Michael. He had just bought a new Maserati, and he invited me to drive it. Now, I don't love to drive, and I hadn't owned a car in years. Somehow, though, I found it in me to say yes. We were driving along in rural Massachusetts, and it was pretty mellow, not many traffic lights. I was nervous behind the wheel, but I managed. That is, until we approached the store and found only street parking. I pulled up to the curb and heard a sound you never, ever want to hear when you're driving your friend's new Maserati.

"KKKKKKRRRRRRRR…"

I couldn't breathe. I couldn't speak. I was freaking out inside, and on the outside, I was frozen with fear. I was so sure Michael would be angry with me, so I braced myself for the inevitable punishment. Instead, he said, "I forgot to tell you that the profile of this car is wider than most. I'm so sorry."

Now, Michael's gentle temperament is a gift—not everyone would be so kind if you scraped their new car against the curb. At the same time, I noticed that I had an *expectation* that I would be punished. It wasn't too big a leap to see that same expectation was the root cause of my fear of expressing my opinion or allowing my voice the freedom it deserved.

Most of the time, we're held captive in an invisible

prison of our own beliefs. In my marriage, for example, I believed that my husband held all the cards. That belief happened to be true, but only because I *allowed* it. My belief that I was never going to be good enough kept our unhealthy dynamic in place. So, what beliefs are silently running *your* life and holding you back from bursting forth into freedom?

Freedom Involves Play

For so long, I had been so responsible and so hell-bent on people-pleasing that I didn't have much appreciation or reverence for fun. I thought play was a waste of time and that people who engaged in it were lazy or not on a serious path. I have since learned that play is actually vital and healing. What about you? Do you allow yourself to let go and have fun? Or are you using obligation to shelter yourself? What could you do today to invite more joy into your life?

Re-Envision Your Life

Even though Cheryl's words—"allow yourself to fantasize about being divorced"—were hard to hear, she was inviting me to try a powerful visualization exercise. She had been by my side from the very moment the journey began, and I trusted her.

So, I found my breath, and with Cheryl's support, I began to imagine what it would be like to be divorced. In my case, that also meant visualizing what it would be like to no longer be at the mercy of another human being. This exercise allowed me to begin to see a life outside of my marriage—a different life and a new identity. A freer life.

It's somewhat magical, but as soon as you admit to yourself what you already know and tell the truth to someone safe, you'll start to feel a little more space in your internal world. You no longer have to hold yourself so tightly to protect your secrets and placate your fears.

Visualizing myself as divorced gave me a new perspective and allowed me to reframe my situation. It was only then that I could begin to feel excited about the possibilities for my life.

When we start to think differently, the outside world begins to change. Transformation thrusts us into the unfamiliar. We tend to be afraid of the unfamiliar—which we perceive as an abyss—even though the familiar can be uncomfortable or even painful. We are enslaved by our habitual patterns because as lifeless as they may be, they give us a sense of certainty that we crave. But living according to habits is like never trying a new recipe: We miss all the other flavors that are possible.

You don't actually have to *make* the leap in order to reap the benefits of a new possibility. All you have to do is start to visualize different possibilities. By willingly considering what potentialities may exist in the abyss of the unknown, you can begin to imagine yourself free.

Nicole Tells Her Story

I wore a bikini. I wore a bikini on a beach in plain sight of everyone in broad daylight. I realize this doesn't sound like much of an accomplishment. But this was my first time.

I once had a very respectable bikini bod but never had the guts to rock one. I always wanted to wear one, but I was too self-conscious of my scars and my thighs ... and too trusting of my Inner Critic. I mean, she must know what's best for me. She's known me my whole life!

So, three kids, two saggy boobs, and one sad-faced belly button later, I was determined to kick her out of my life and don a stringy little reggae number I found at the store. In the weeks before, I had one of those moments when I realized that ego wasn't about arrogance. It was about living on the outskirts of an authentic life and denying myself my own love. I saw that the Inner Critic I so trusted was actually the voice of my ego, whose mission was keeping my mind preoccupied with the small stuff and away from the real show. So, I began to shut her down.

Fast forward to the day ... I shed the last of the forty pounds of baby weight, but still had more stretch marks than could be counted and a body, though mostly in shape, that wasn't quite the shape you see in magazines. But that was okay! Had I held on to my low self-concept, I would have sat in my cute enough tankini wishing I had the ovaries to get my Marley on. Instead, I took off my cover-up, revealing my red, black, and gold to the world. And guess what? The earth stayed in orbit.

I actually forgot about what I was wearing and just enjoyed the beach. It wasn't about who looked like what. It was about being fully there. I watched my little girl boogie board in her bikini, I inhaled the salt air, and I silently prayed she'd always have that two-piece 'tude.

So, yeah, on the surface, it doesn't sound like much—putting on a bikini. But that day, I won a personal thirty-nine-year battle and moved toward an authentic self-concept that can't be cultivated by planting my roots in pop culture's shifting sands. It must be grown in the rich soil built by living my own truth and accepting whatever that may be. This shift in my thinking is an ongoing process. That itsy-bitsy, teeny-weeny, Rasta-striped string bikini was the first major mile marker I reached while walking away from my critical self and toward self-love. Freedom can be found in a bathing suit. Who knew?

What Does *Your* Freedom Look Like?

1. I had to anesthetize myself emotionally to some degree in order to stay in the life that wasn't working for me. I was attached to an identity that put me in a box. Review your character descriptions from step one, and write down your answers to these questions:

   - Where in my life do I feel constricted?
   - Where do I need more freedom in my life?
   - In what ways has my current identity put me in a box?
   - What restrictions do I feel as a result of the identity I put out into the world?

2. By staying bound to my marriage, I could avoid moving into the fullness of my life. I could keep up the tense charade of perfection. Trying to be a heroine was a drug for me. What about you? Ask yourself these questions, and write down your answers:

    - How does not being free serve me?
    - The benefits or payoffs I receive from staying bound in my current situation are

      _____

    - These benefits or payoffs allow me to avoid

      _____

    - Without these benefits or payoffs, I would be free to _____

3. If you allow yourself to be free, you will have to give up these benefits. What fears come up when you think of letting go of them?

    If I were free, I'm afraid _____
    If I were free, I'm afraid _____
    If I were free, I'm afraid _____

4. When we push aside parts of ourselves that we don't like or that frighten us, we expend a lot of energy. What we push away only becomes stronger, louder, and more insistent. It's important to honor and integrate all of these parts of ourselves because when we accept them, they no longer need our attention so much. What parts of you have you shut off, and what parts of you are longing to be expressed? Freedom means learning to love the totality of who we are—both the dark and the light.

The parts of me that I dislike most are

_____

The parts of me that frighten me most are

_____

The parts of me that I'd set free if I weren't afraid are _____

5. Who would you be if you were no longer living a life that you feel is "acceptable" and safe—if you were living your free, authentic life? Review the character descriptions you created in step one. Write a description of the "you" who is living this free, authentic life without fear or the need for secrets.

6. What is required for you to imagine yourself free? What do you have to surrender in order to be free? Joseph Campbell said, "We must be willing to let go of the life we planned so as to have the life that is waiting for us."

In order to be free, I must let go of

_____

In order to be free, I must change

_____

7. Now that you have explored your restrictions, ask yourself this fundamental question: What does freedom mean to me?

Close your eyes, and imagine what freedom would feel like. Allow yourself to be surprised by what you envision. You are living freely. What are you doing? How does it feel in your body? What possibilities do you see if you let go of all of the stories about what "can't be"? What would your life look like if no one could criticize or praise you?

Experience your visualization with all of your senses and in the future tense. Allow it to be expansive, like a child might imagine it. Paint a picture in your mind. How is this free life different from the life you're living right now? Caution: Don't try to figure out the logistics of your free life. We get stuck when we try to figure out "how" we will create something new. For now, only think about the "what," not the "how." Focus solely on desire, sensation, and possibility.

Write down what you see and feel in your visualization so that you have a record of it. Then, ask yourself: Once I have made this change, I will feel freer, and I will feel

_____.

Allow yourself to bathe and bask in your fantasy of freedom because it will become the basis of the new life you will create for yourself. Every day, spend at least two minutes imagining yourself free. You can do it while you're taking a shower so that it doesn't take extra time. (The shower, it turns out, is a magical time when many important ideas can come to mind!) The more you allow yourself to visualize, the more real your vision will be, and the closer it will be to reality.

A MOMENT TO FORGIVE

It's important to honor where you've been and even honor the fears that have kept you restricted. Those fears developed during childhood, and their job was to protect you. The problem is that they protect you *too well* once you reach adulthood.

Take a moment to forgive the parts of you that have worked hard to protect you and have inadvertently held you back as a result. As you begin to disengage their stronghold, they will try harder to keep you in check. Rather than meet these parts of you with anger, meet them with compassion. That expression of love will make it easier to move into a life of greater freedom.

Step Four
Make One Different Choice

Garbage bags. White ones with red drawstrings. There were nearly a dozen of them, filled with my belongings and stuffed into the Suburban. On February 25, 2009, ten months after my husband read the journals, he kicked me out of the house for the first time. In a rage, he did the packing and sent me on my way. It was my birthday.

It was the first, but not the last time he kicked me out of the house. (The house that, incidentally, I had bought and paid for.) In the two years after my husband confronted me about the affair, he kicked me out five times.

Five times, but I only returned four. The fifth time was January 12, 2010. It was the culmination of several leavings.

We had agreed on a separation—three months to start, after which we'd assess whether we needed another three months. He was unwilling to actually separate, however, and was constantly engaging me in any and every possible way. It got to the point that I just couldn't continue the dysfunctional cycle any longer. I told him I wanted no contact for thirty days, and that if he got in touch before the agreed-upon date it would automatically mean another thirty days of no contact.

Drawing that line in the sand was very difficult for me, but it empowered me to begin to take control of my life.

Ironically, when I began to take back control, at first it felt like I was *losing* control. I was outside of my comfort zone and had no idea what to expect. Eventually, I learned that it's an illusion to think we're in control. We're actually *less* in control when we hold rigidly to the familiar. In that case, we're enslaved by fear. We are not free to move with the pulse of life. When we let go into the arms of the unfamiliar, on the other hand, we enter the flow. We can follow our truth and our desire, creating the kind of life we most want—a life filled with possibility and enjoyment rather than tension and terror.

Too frequently, we think we're choosing peace and comfort over freedom. But in truth, we're sacrificing our inner peace in hopes of outer peace. That outer peace is, more often than not, dictated by someone else and not by our own needs. In my case, I sacrificed my own well-being and happiness for peace with my husband. But no matter how hard I tried, I still didn't achieve peace with him. So, I had *no* peace—neither outer nor inner.

Choosing comfort meant I had to go back to the same pattern over and over. I already knew the outcome of that pattern, and it wasn't good. Not until I made a different choice could I design a new ending to my story.

Break Free of Negative Patterns

Making one different choice can have an enormous impact as you move toward jumping into your new, better life. It's the starting point that leads you to the next steps.

When you do one thing differently, you break a

pattern and prove to yourself that there is life beyond the familiar. I'm not going to pretend that breaking patterns is always a smooth process; often, it's anything but. My husband was hardly happy that I was no longer playing our game.

Our game went like this: He kicked me out, and I went back to him. Once I showed him that I wasn't playing anymore, he was, of course, outraged.

Remember what David Whyte said—if you are living the life you are meant to live, it is inevitable that someone will feel betrayed. We can't give our lives away to avoid someone else's anger, demands, or needs. I did that for much too long, and it practically killed me. I had to do something different regardless of the outcome.

As I have said, for a long time I thought divorce wasn't possible for me. I was too frightened of the consequences if I left. It seemed unfathomable to go through the exposure of having done something terrible. But eventually, I had to face my terror and my shame. And guess what? It didn't annihilate me. The ground didn't crumble beneath me. I'm still standing ... and I have more personal power today than I ever thought possible. If I can do that, so can you.

And it all started with that one different choice.

Here's another simple example of making a different choice. While on my way to Miraval Resort in Tucson, Arizona, for their annual retreat with Louise Hay and Cheryl Richardson, the craziest thing happened—I missed my flight! For the first time ever in my whole life! It was just so unlike me.

I was there in plenty of time, but the Denver airport was a zoo because of spring break. The lines were so long that by the time I got up to the kiosk counter, I was too late to check in for my flight. A frazzled airline worker pointed me toward another serpentine line for rebooking.

I *had* to get to Miraval, so I called my travel agent (a.k.a., my travel angel) and asked him if he could move faster than this line. Sure enough, he was able to grab the last seat on the last available flight to Tucson that day. It was departing at 10:00 p.m.

It was 10:00 a.m. Oy.

Plus, there was a $1,100 change fee.

Plus, I *still* had to stand in that slow-moving line so a customer service rep could make the change official. It was not a good moment.

I was in line for more than an hour, surrounded by people bitching and kids screaming. But for some reason, I decided not to be upset. I decided to walk my talk, and do one thing differently. I channeled Cheryl and Louise, and I waited patiently with a positive attitude. When I finally got to the counter, I smiled and said to the agent, "I'm determined to be your kindest customer today!" The frazzled agent next to her looked at me like I was a bit crazy.

"You already are," she said. "And I'm sure that by the end of our shift, you still will be."

She successfully booked me on the 10:00 p.m. flight. "Do you know this will cost $1,100?" she asked.

"Yes, I know," I answered.

Well, positivity is apparently infectious. Since I had been so nice and so calm, she told me, she was going to bypass the fee in the system and not charge me a dime. Wow! Just doing that one thing differently—being kind instead of complaining—saved me $1,100!

She also put me on standby for the 2:30 p.m. flight, and I was first on the list. What could have spiraled into an "Ain't it awful?" day actually became quite joyful.

And happily, I found myself tucked into the last available seat on the 2:30 flight, had a great chat with someone on the way to the resort, and made it to Miraval in time for dinner.

One Choice Leads to Another

Making that first different choice gave me permission to make another new choice in my life—visualizing quitting my job. It wasn't that I didn't enjoy the work—quite the contrary, it was my dream job—but there was just so much of it! I couldn't see a way out of the stress and overwhelm beyond leaving Hay House.

Around that time, I was taking a walk in Melbourne, Australia, with my boss and close friend, Reid Tracy, the President of Hay House. I suddenly realized that my whole quest for "gold stars" had to end. I admitted to Reid that I felt overworked and overwhelmed. I even confessed that I'd been fantasizing about quitting.

"I sensed that you were at the end of your rope," he said, "but you don't have to quit your job. You just have to stop holding yourself to such unrealistic expectations. Support is available if you'd only take it!"

Support? What was *that*? I was not a woman who asked for support.

"It's not about your indispensability at work," Reid continued. "It's about your irreplaceability as a human."

Woah. He was right. My individuality can never be replaced by anyone else. It's about who I am, not what I do. I had been living in a long-running story that everyone loved me because of what I did for them. The truth was that people loved me simply because *they loved me*. When he made that statement, it dawned on me: My workaholism was driven by my *ego*. I had bought into the belief that I was "the only one" who could get things done because some part of me *wanted to believe it*. I thought that my Superwoman persona "earned" me my right to be alive. No one else required me to go to such lengths. I was the only one who felt I had to do so in order to be loved, to be acceptable.

But the truth is that even if I do absolutely nothing for the rest of my life—accumulate no more gold stars—I will still be loved. What a revelation!

I used to think love would come from the outside in, but I know now that it must grow from the inside first. No amount of external validation will ever match my internal expression of self-love, self-forgiveness, and self-acceptance. All the gold stars in the world cannot earn me the recognition that can only be found within my own heart.

Essentially, what Reid said to me caused the clouds to part. Suddenly, I felt free to do the most outrageous thing imaginable: delegate! It was as if he gave me permission to give *myself* permission. That one different choice—delegation—paved the way for me to stay in my job and continue to do what I love without burning out.

And guess what happened when I stopped seeking out those gold stars? The gold stars kept coming! Even after I had let go of my standard of perfection. Know that you will receive accolades for one reason and one reason only: for being you. You are lovable for who you are.

I can't say that I'm forever cured of the Gold-Star Disease. I think it will probably be with me for the rest of my life. But today, I'm much more aware when it creeps in, and I can make better choices each time it rears its head.

Elizabeth Tells Her Story

I grew up being taught to be there for my mother over myself. I was there at her every beck and call, and seeking her approval was my life's mission growing up. Lacking a sense of my own self, being there for her gave me a purpose, a reason for being. I did anything to please her, but it was never enough.

It eventually drained me of life energy for living my own life and believing in myself. I wanted to be a therapist; she wanted me to be a teacher. So, I went to school to be a teacher.

As the years went by and I grew older, resentment grew inside me. At the age of twenty, I moved away from my home state of California to Colorado, thinking that putting distance between us would allow me some separation. But, of course, as the old saying goes, "Wherever you go, there you are." I heard her voice constantly in my head telling me what I should and shouldn't do

The distance helped, along with the fact that she was busy with her own life for many years, but everything changed when her second husband died. Suddenly, I was back at the center of her attention, expected to be the center of her life and be there for her in a way she could not be there for herself.

The Christmas following her husband's death, she came to visit me and my now growing family. At the time, I was struggling with a preteen son and confided my struggles with my mother. One evening, I watched as my mother sat with my oldest son watching a movie and heard her asking him how he could be so stupid for thinking the way he did. To my horror, I realized that she was treating my son the way that she had treated me when I was growing up. I was mortified at the fact that I did nothing to stop this emotional abuse, and at the same time, I felt powerless to stop it. I was frozen in fear both for my son and for myself. I did the only thing I knew to do, which was keep quiet.

A couple of weeks after her visit, we spoke on the phone, and she proceeded to tell me how disappointed she was with my son. She said, "You know, I am glad you are struggling. Now you know how I felt!"

How could my own mother wish pain on me, just to have her own experience validated?! In that moment, I made the choice to exit my mother's life. I sat down and wrote her a letter, telling her that I needed to remove myself from her life for the time being to resolve some things. Putting that letter in the mailbox was literally like jumping off a cliff for me. That decision, doing that one thing differently, became the biggest turning point in my life.

I knew the risk I was taking would have consequences, and the worst thing I could imagine came to pass. My mother called me the evening she received the letter, leaving a message begging me to reconsider. The next morning, she called and left another message, saying, "Have a nice life." As I suspected, she disowned me. But instead of feeling sad, I felt relieved to be free from the bondage I had allowed myself to be controlled by my entire life. I entered Codependence Anonymous and started a journey into myself, discovering what it was that made me feel the need to accommodate and please my mother at the cost of my own soul.

In the two years that followed, I took my life back. I went back to school and eventually became a counselor. I embraced me instead of her for the first time in my life.

The real miracle is that I not only took my life back, but my mother got her life back as well. She did not remarry and learned to stand on her own two feet. We have a semblance of a relationship today while I remain fully intact. I learned that it is possible to be in a relationship and not abandon myself. And the greatest gift of all is that this has become my life's work. Empowering women to take their lives back and be all of who they are while in relationship with others is a passion that fuels my life.

Your Different Choice

What in your life would you like to change? For me, divorce seemed like too big a step at first. It would have been too big a leap for me to tell my husband I wanted to leave, even after he'd kicked me out that last time. But I *could* make one different choice—the choice to take some time off instead of going right back to him. That choice inched me closer to being able to ultimately ask for a divorce.

Sometimes, you have to tiptoe an inch at a time toward a new life. That's okay. Each step you take will give you more courage.

Bear in mind that there will be repercussions when you make a different choice. Like in Elizabeth's situation, other people in your life may be unhappy to see you grow. They know that it could mean you're growing away from them, leaving them behind, and they may fear losing you. Or they might feel jealous to see you move forward in places where they remain stuck. When you do, you hold a mirror up to them. Watching you make changes and free yourself may trigger how trapped they feel in their own lives. They might feel more comfortable trying to pull you back. In Australia, they call this "tall-poppy syndrome"—the tallest poppy gets cut down.

But *you* get to decide. How willing are you to let someone else dictate your life? What are the costs of staying in situations that no longer serve you?

When you choose to do even one thing differently, you take a step toward disassembling structures you have had in place for a while—maybe many years. You may find yourself staring at a pile of rubble for a period of time. But eventually, you will begin to rebuild. A little rubble never hurt anybody.

If your life were a house, would it have been condemned long ago? If so, it's time to make a different choice.

In my experience, the sky doesn't usually fall to the degree we expect. So, take a moment to question your assumptions. Have you blown the stakes out of proportion? I definitely had. I was terrified of certain people knowing about my affair, but they ended up being much more empathetic than I ever expected. I just had to embrace the possibility of temporary chaos. I had to let it be okay that I might not be on steady ground for a little while. Just like building a new home, the difficulty turned out to be worth it.

I discovered that if you aim your compass at chaos, a map will present itself.

You can anchor yourself by continuing to talk to someone safe and visualizing your new life. Also, continue the simple rituals that you don't feel the need to change—like enjoying your usual cup of coffee in the morning, exercising in nature, watching your favorite television show, or relaxing with a good friend.

For now, you only have to do one thing differently. And it doesn't have to be earth-shattering.

For example, I have a client, Celeste, whose husband likes her to be in bed when he wakes up in the morning. Yet Celeste goes to sleep much earlier than he does and likes to be up early to write or exercise. She had been acquiescing to his wishes for years, even though it made her crazy and caused her to miss the time to herself. As a result, she began to resent her husband for being so demanding. Ultimately, she realized that she was enabling him to be this way by not standing up for her own needs for fear that he would be angry or withhold love from her.

A few weeks into our coaching relationship, she wanted to address this and have me hold her accountable to change her behavior and the situation. No matter how much fear she experienced and how uncomfortable it made her feel, she committed to getting out of bed when she wanted one morning a week to do whatever she wanted to do. Then, she committed to two mornings. Over time, she has created the inner strength and courage to decide each morning when she wakes if she wants to get up and out and do her own thing or if she wants to stay in bed and greet her husband when he wakes. It's true that we teach people how to treat us and that when we stand firmly in our truth and make certain needs non-negotiable, we create a new cycle of acceptance for ourselves and others.

The Change Needs to Be a Challenge

Remember George Costanza on the TV show *Seinfeld*? In one episode, he did the opposite of what he would normally do and found that the results were much better than usual. For example, rather than pretend he was someone he wasn't, he approached a woman and immediately admitted that he was unemployed and lived with his parents. To his surprise, she responded positively to his honesty. While I don't recommend trying something as outrageous as that, I suggest you pick one thing as an experiment and try doing the opposite of what you would normally do.

While what you change doesn't have to be earth-shattering, don't let the fear of repercussions cause you to choose something that is *too* easy. For example, changing your brand of coffee may be making a different choice, but it won't be empowering enough to propel you forward. (I say this as I cling, body and soul, to my daily Caffe D'Vita espresso!) Pick something that feels at least a little bit edgy.

Turn Off Your Autopilot

1. Write about one change you can make in your routine that will immediately open you up to different possibilities. Where are you on autopilot in a way that does not serve you? For example, you might choose to save both money and calories

by giving up a food that you know isn't good for you. Again, if this is too easy for you to do, choose something that will challenge you at least to some degree.

2. As I have said, we tend to move toward commitments that we have made unconsciously. Once you have decided what one change you will make, write down your *conscious* commitment to make that change.

    I commit to changing _____

3. What fears do you have about making the change?

    If I do _____,
    then _____ could happen.
      How rational are these fears? If you think your fears are likely to come true, think about how you will manage any repercussions from the change you make.
      If you worry that someone in your life will react with anger or extreme emotion, can you visualize this person acting differently? Take a moment to send loving energy to this individual. Have a conversation in your mind with his or her higher self about what you want, and ask for openness and understanding.

4. Write down an "excuse inventory." Completely empty your brain of all of the reasons you tell yourself you cannot make this change. Take some time with this to make sure you really think of everything. Then burn your list.

5. What positive results do you see happening as a result of doing this one thing differently?

    I am excited to _____

A New Choice For a New Path

Yes, this step is about doing one thing differently, but it's actually about building a muscle. You're learning how to make different choices on an ongoing basis, every day, for the rest of your life. Making new and possibly dangerous choices is required if you want to live a sustainably satisfying life. When your "change muscle" becomes stronger, you are less likely to get stuck in circumstances that hold you back or keep you small. If you know how to make little changes, you can make adjustments as you go and follow a dynamic path based on courage and freedom.

If your past choices got you to the present, your present choices will take you into the future. Learning how to choose differently makes that brighter future possible. So, try it! Make one different choice, and see how your life changes. As motivational speaker Les Brown says, "Life has no limitations except the ones you make."

A MOMENT TO FORGIVE

Think about the patterns in your life that have caused you pain. Do you feel frustrated that you've let them go on so long? Do you have judgments about yourself because of them? Do you blame others—like your parents, your partner, or your boss—for those patterns? Take a moment to breathe and forgive yourself and others for any negative patterns that have played out in your life. Honor those patterns for teaching you what you need to know in order to move forward from the moment of now.

Step Five
Set Your New Boundaries

"Sit on the floor," my therapist said. I looked at her skeptically. Had she lost her marbles? But she was patiently waiting for me to do as I was told, so I slowly skootched off the couch and onto the carpet.

She handed me a long piece of rope and told me to make a boundary around myself, illustrating my own personal space.

Without thinking too hard, I hugged my knees tightly into my chest and made myself as small as possible before circling the rope as close to my body as I could.

Wow, this was a very telling exercise! Clearly, I didn't have any boundaries. The reality was right there in front of me—or around me—and I couldn't deny it any longer. I was willing to be violated if it served or pleased someone else.

I'm a big fan of the Enneagram personality typing system. If you know it at all, you'll know what it means when I say I'm a type 3—the Achiever. We strive to be the best, and in the process become highly adept at morphing into what other people want. "You need me to be Miss Super Efficient? No problem!" "You need me to be your savior? No problem!"

I'm hardly alone here. Most of us don't know how to set boundaries. We're taught to put others ahead of ourselves. (This is especially true for women, but there are plenty of men who have the same issue.) At a workshop, Cheryl once said something that stuck with

me: "If I spend my life pleasing people, I spend my life."
Up until that point, I definitely had been spending my
life. I was just about bankrupt when I finally woke up.

Not everyone puts others ahead of themselves, of
course, and some of us are more prone to people-
pleasing than others. But the attachment many of us
feel to keeping others happy is pretty tenacious. In a
certain way, pleasing becomes our currency—the way
we purchase love and attention. If we don't think we
inherently deserve love, we feel we must find some way
to earn it.

I used to spend so much time reacting and responding
to everyone else that my life had no direction.
Other people's lives, problems, and wants set the
course for my life. Once I realized it was okay for
me to think about and identify what I wanted,
remarkable things began to take place in my life.
—Melody Beattie, author of *Codependent No More*

The Birth of My First Boundary

Not going back to my husband the last time he kicked
me out of the house—that one thing I did differently—
was the first boundary I had ever set with him. But it
was more than that: It was the first boundary I'd set
with *anyone* in my entire life. It was the first time I ever
thought purely about my own needs, the first time I ever
chose myself over another person. It was huge.

And that one step inspired me to set more
boundaries. Necessary ones. As I mentioned earlier, I
eventually told my husband that I wanted four weeks

straight of no contact whatsoever—no emails, no voicemails, no Facebook messages. I also told him that I would not respond to threats—period. (Unfortunately, it had come to that.) It was so difficult for me to send that email to him that Cheryl and Debbie literally had to help my finger press "send" on my laptop. Setting such a firm boundary was not in my repertoire.

It was just two weeks before my husband started emailing and calling me again. Empowered by the boundary I had set in my first email, I sent him another stating that the four-week period would start over every time he contacted me. I gave him the date, time, and number to call a month later when I would have my therapist on the line with us on a conference call. I also let him know that I would not speak with him again unless a third party was present.

Leaving my marriage and getting him out of my head felt like what I imagine it might feel like to leave a cult. As my mind began to clear and settle, and as my habit of reactivity and walking on eggshells began to lessen and loosen, setting boundaries became easier.

On the day we were scheduled to reconnect, he did not call the conference line at the appointed time. Instead, he called my cell phone and left repeated voicemails. The messages started soft and sweet and built to full-blown rage and threats when I didn't respond. Gratefully, Cheryl and my sister had made a pact to listen to his voicemails for me and only relay what I absolutely needed to know. This prevented the toxicity from entering my system and weakening my resolve.

With their help, I was able to stick to my guns. On June 15, 2010—another date I will never forget—I decided I was never going back.

The months that followed were a blur. I filed for divorce, met with lawyers, went through a painfully long mediation, agreed to a settlement, and got the dissolution decree. During all of that time, my husband and I never spoke or saw one another. I was finally able to set a boundary—and keep it.

Having set my own boundaries for the first time, I was no longer reacting or responding to someone else. I was suddenly able to act from a clean, clear place. It was amazing. But while I felt stronger in some ways, I also felt like a young colt trying to walk for the first time—which is fitting, since I was indeed birthing a new identity. My legs felt gangly, like I could barely stand. Of course, I did learn to stand on my own two feet again, and this book is a testament to that. It took some time, but it happened eventually.

So, take heart! When you set new boundaries, you may at first feel as though you have a new pair of legs. You might feel off balance, but it won't last forever. Yes, it can be very scary to operate from a place of what you want, especially when you're a people-pleaser like me. As children, we learn to respond in a way that brings us the least stress and trouble—and that often means allowing ourselves to be moved by others' wants and needs. But as adults, we have to learn to get past our ingrained fears and make clear choices.

Many of us have an inner dialogue that tells us we're not enough, that we're not lovable. Refusing to set healthy boundaries is one of the primary ways we express that belief. If we want to live fulfilled lives, however, we have to let go of the belief that the needs and opinions of others are more important or valid than our own. We have to stop taking it personally when someone disagrees with us. We have to stop believing that if we disagree with someone or ask for what we want, we'll end up alone and unloved.

"You're the only thinker inside your head."

Louise Hay said this to me while I was going through my divorce. It's so obvious, but the first time she said it to me, I had one of those "a-ha" moments. I realized that I had given away this privilege to the people around me, allowing them "real estate" in my head. It's so easy to forget that we get to make our own choices for our own lives. If we allow someone else's beliefs to invade our heads, it's up to us to disengage from those voices and find our own. Who is taking up space in your head, and how can you set the boundaries you need in order to have the inner peace you deserve?

The Balance between Me and Them

I realize that you may have children, and your responsibilities as a parent may legitimately preclude you from setting certain boundaries or making certain choices. Fair enough. But that doesn't mean there are *no* boundaries to be set. Check in to see whether you're making excuses so that you can stay in the realm of the familiar. If so, take the time to evaluate your life honestly. Do you truly not have choices available to you? Imagine a compromise you might come to that would allow you to set a healthy boundary. If you can't think of one on your own, consult with a trusted friend. Because it *is* possible to make changes in the direction of your dreams without necessarily abandoning your obligations and responsibilities.

People often use their children or their money issues as excuses for not setting boundaries and taking care of themselves. Just as they instruct you on a plane, remember to put on your own oxygen mask first. Remember that your children learn how to be healthy adults from the example you set. You'll teach them a lot by striking a balance between how much you give them and how well you take care of yourself. You might not be able to do everything you'd like, but it doesn't mean you can't do *anything*.

As Cheryl Richardson says, let go of "A-to-Z" thinking. A-to-Z thinking is all or nothing; it assumes that if you can't make it to Z, you can't have anything at all. But it doesn't always have to be an either/or proposition. You only have to get from A to B. Small shifts add up.

It's like going on a diet. If you cheat and eat an entire container of Talenti Sea Salt Caramel gelato (not that I'm admitting anything), you might feel so defeated that you give up on the diet entirely. The truth is that you cheated once. It was one day. The next day, you can start again.

So, if you're prone to A-to-Z thinking, evaluate your situation thoroughly and ask yourself: What steps *can* I take to start toward the boundary that I'd like to set? For example, where might I say no when I would otherwise say yes? Where can I ask for what I really want instead of dumbing down my request to please another person?

Take Off the Cape

If you're like me, the habit of trying to take care of everyone else will be a tough one to break. For me, creating a new identity after my divorce allowed me to no longer be defined by heroic achievements. What a relief to relinquish the image of perfection I had been projecting out to the world! I took off my Superwoman cape and finally broke free from the persona I'd created to get validation.

Perhaps you, too, are soaring around, searching for love. Whatever the intention is beneath your need, know that you are not alone. Start slowly. First, try just tucking the superhero cape inside your shirt for a day or two. You don't have to take it all the way off! Your ego will do its damnedest to pull it back out (to hell with boundaries!) and that's okay. Just keep reminding yourself that you're ready to start rescuing yourself instead of everyone else.

And if you're like me, one day you'll forget all about that cape. You'll be cleaning out your closet and you'll find it hiding back there between your winter parka and your raincoat. And you'll smile. You'll remember the thrill of being a superhero, but you won't need that identity anymore. Somewhere along the way, through some miracle, you will have become comfortable with being exactly who you are—with all your positive and negative qualities.

Healthy Boundaries as a Way of Life

Setting that one boundary helped me to develop the courage to set more boundaries—well beyond my relationship with my husband. About that time, a friend called me up and said, "I'm having a terrible day. I need you to do something to make me happy."

Before I knew what was coming out of my mouth, I said, "Unfortunately, I'm no longer in the business of making other people happy."

I was half mortified I'd said that, but I was also proud. It was an important moment. By saying no when I needed to take care of myself, I was free to later choose—from a full-hearted place—to help my friend feel better if I *wanted* to do so. But it wasn't my "job" to do that for her anymore.

As they say, nothing pours from an empty pitcher. We have to fill our own pitchers first. Otherwise, we are only giving out of obligation—not from our true desire—and that inevitably leads to resentment.

Another situation—this time on the job—showed me how much further I had to go with my boundary-setting. I was producing two back-to-back live events with Wayne Dyer over the course of a weekend. He spoke in Atlanta on Saturday afternoon, and then the whole crew flew to Detroit where he was to speak again on Sunday afternoon. At 10:00 p.m. Saturday night, once we were all settled into our hotel rooms in Detroit, my phone rang. It was Wayne, and he was in a panic.

"My briefcase," he told me. "I can't find it! I'm sure I left it somewhere en route from Atlanta."

Everything was in that briefcase—his notes and books for his lecture, notes for the next book he was writing, his money, and more. He couldn't even *think* about getting on stage the next day without it.

At that point in my life I was still chasing those gold stars, seeking all of my validation externally. I was going to figure out how to get that briefcase if it killed me!

I thought back: We'd left the stage in Atlanta and climbed immediately into a van to the airport, so he'd had his briefcase then. I had a hunch it was still in that vehicle. I called the car company and was told that the van wouldn't be back to the lot for another hour.

When I called an hour later, the news wasn't good. The dispatcher told me he'd checked, and the briefcase wasn't there. I begged him to go back out and look again. It was dark out, I figured, so maybe he'd just missed it. I sat on hold, praying it was hiding under a seat. Lo and behold, I was right! The dispatcher came back and told me he had the briefcase in hand.

By now, though, it was close to midnight. Wayne called me again, and I told him I'd located the briefcase and was working on getting it to Detroit.

"Go to bed, and don't worry," I told him. He was relieved and appreciative, but still anxious.

I asked the car company if they would put an employee on a plane first thing in the morning to deliver the briefcase. No such luck—traveling with someone else's bag had become illegal after the 9/11 terrorist attack. I called FedEx, UPS, DHL, and every other carrier I could find in the phone book, but everyone was off the clock for the weekend. I called other airlines to ask about freight and cargo shipments. Once again, it was a no-go because it was a Saturday night. I called my travel agent, but even putting our heads together, we couldn't come up with a way to get the briefcase from Atlanta to Detroit by 2:00 p.m. when Wayne was supposed to walk on stage.

I had a reputation for achieving the impossible. I had set my own bar so high that even though it was the wee hours of the morning and I had no idea what to do, failure was still not an option. At 4:00 a.m. I got dressed, walked downstairs, and asked the bellman to get me a taxi. In the back seat, on my laptop, I bought a round-trip ticket to Atlanta. I sent emails to my staff with instructions for setting up at the venue and getting the event going without me. We were expecting 2,000 people, and I wouldn't get there until about thirty minutes before show time.

Based on my experiences that day, I believe that Detroit and Atlanta are the biggest airports in the whole world. I had to go through security, get to my departure gate in Detroit, fly, go out to baggage claim in Atlanta where a guy from the car company was waiting for me, retrieve the briefcase, go back through security (where they questioned and groped me because I had only just arrived in Atlanta minutes before and was traveling with only a briefcase), get to my departure gate, fly again, get out of the Detroit airport, hop into a taxi, and get to the event venue on time.

As I sat on the plane, preparing to take off for Detroit, I made a phone call.

"Hi, Wayne. I've got your briefcase."

"Where are you?"

"That's not important."

"You're not in Detroit, are you?"

"You'll have your briefcase before you go on stage."

"Nancy, did you do something crazy?'

"Wayne, just go to your Bikram Yoga class, and I'll see you soon."

I got to the venue just a few minutes before Wayne's car pulled up. As he stepped out of the car, with throngs of fans surrounding us, I smiled and extended my arm with briefcase in hand. Jokingly, he put up his hand as if to dismiss the offer.

"Oh, I don't need *that!*" he said.

Without missing a beat, in front of all those people, I flipped off the father of motivation.

We have a little ritual when I introduce Wayne on stage. The last thing I say is, "I know he needs no introduction, but please welcome to the stage one of my most favorite men in the world—Wayne Dyer." He then comes on, the crowd goes wild, he gives me a hug, and I whisper, "Have fun!" in his ear.

That day, however, he held on to me so that I couldn't walk offstage. He turned and told the audience the whole story. He explained that there was nothing I wouldn't do, at any cost, to make whatever needed to happen *happen*. He even told them about how I had flipped him off.

Now, that might sound like a story of triumph, and I suppose in a way it is. But at what cost? As Wayne put it on the phone, it was a bit "crazy." I was motivated by the belief that I had to "make whatever needed to happen *happen*" in order to have a right to be in the world. I compulsively sought those gold stars because I didn't think I could be loved otherwise. Again, I did it because I thought I would only be loved for what I *did,* not for *who I was*.

That extreme experience showed me the need to relax and begin to love myself for who I am—flaws and all—and give myself what I need internally rather than hunt for it externally. I still have to remind myself of this lesson quite often, but as I've said, I'm much better now at catching myself before I go chasing gold stars.

How can we embrace rest and play if we've tied our self-worth to what we produce?
—Brené Brown

Amy Tells Her Story

My coach gave me an exercise where I had to actively disappoint someone every day for two weeks. Actively disappoint—that meant looking for people to say no to.

It's not an exaggeration to say I felt physically sick undertaking this.

At first, I disappointed my husband. I'd told him I'd cook dinner one evening. Then, early in the afternoon, I called him to say I was no longer going to make dinner. Either he could cook or we could get takeaway or eat out. I was so nervous doing this, my tummy was going over and I felt like crying. The big news is he didn't give a sh**. He said, "No worries, Babe; I'll sort something out for us."

I was so surprised at how okay people were with me when I disappointed them! It got easier, and by day three I was actively disappointing several people. I emailed my coach and told her she had created a monster! For the first time, I felt that I was living my life on my terms.

It facilitated the big jump I would make: I went away with my husband for Christmas rather than spend it with my family. Then I walked away from a big project I was halfway through last year because it no longer felt right, and I recently fired two clients that were no longer a fit.

By saying no to making dinner when I didn't want to, I was able to say no to a family Christmas and no to a project and clients that didn't feel right.

Starting small with boundaries has helped me tackle the really big ones, and I have reclaimed my life.

Your New Self-Love Map: Setting Your Boundaries

1. Make a list of what you want, but don't yet have, in different areas of your life. Make sure to include work life, home life, relationships, health, finances, spiritual path, and any other areas that are important to you.

2. Make a list of what you will never tolerate again in your life. For me, this list included my husband's threats and demands, as well as my own need to overachieve.

3. How would you like to strengthen boundaries in various areas of your life?

    > I want to strengthen my boundaries around health by _____

    > I want to strengthen my boundaries around finances by _____

    > I want to strengthen my boundaries around relationships by _____

    > I want to strengthen my boundaries around fun by _____

    > I want to strengthen my boundaries around _____ by _____

4. Choose three of these boundaries that you are willing to set in different areas of your life *this week*. Commit to making these changes. In some

cases, you might have to declare your boundary to someone else, such as "I'm not going to pick you up from work every day." In other cases, you may just take a different action to set your boundary.

The three boundaries I will set this week are:

1. _____
2. _____
3. _____

5. If you worry about someone else's reaction to a boundary you have set, try the exercise from step three in which you speak in your mind to the person's higher self, requesting understanding, reason, and compassion. Then offer the same to this individual when you declare your boundary. If you can remain calm, it will be easier for the other person to stay calm, too. Practice what you will say in the mirror or to a trusted friend, if necessary, in order to keep your composure.

6. After one of my presentations, a woman came up to me and said that she would never be able to leave her husband because he can't live without her. He may believe that, but his belief doesn't make it true. If you need to set a boundary with an adult who is very dependent upon you, try visualizing that you have an invisible thread connecting your solar plexus (the flat area in the center of your torso, between your bottom ribs) with the solar plexus of this person. Imagine what it would be like to cut that thread, and visualize placing your loved one in the arms of his/her higher self. Is it frightening? Do you feel like you're abandoning him/her? If you have an

attachment to someone else that is dysfunctional, this exercise is a way that you can begin to disengage from that attachment so that both of you can grow into the independent people you're meant to be.

You're On Your Way!

As you begin to set boundaries, remember that you're walking yourself to the edge of the cliff where you're preparing to jump. Each time you set a healthy boundary, you say yes to more freedom. Take a deep breath, and commit once again to having the courage to jump into your future.

A MOMENT TO FORGIVE

Take the time right now to forgive yourself for not having set enough boundaries in your life up to this point and for possibly withholding from yourself or not giving yourself as much as you have given others.

At the same time, forgive anyone who has infringed upon your boundaries due to their own issues, and make a commitment to strive for a greater balance between giving to yourself and giving to others.

Step Six
Ask for Help

I'm barely 5'3" tall—and that's if my hair is puffy. Yet, the old me would have climbed up a ladder to grab something from the top shelf rather than ask for help, even if someone tall enough to reach was standing right next to me.

Why was it so hard for me to ask for help? Because I thought that asking for help meant something it didn't.

In April 2010, I was out to dinner with Louise, Cheryl, and Reid after our "Speak, Write, Promote: Become a Mover and Shaker" event in Boston. Even though at that point I had been separated from my husband for three months, I had not revealed to Louise and Reid what was going on in my marriage. They were expecting my husband to be at the event, and I knew they would wonder why he wasn't there. The time had come for me to tell them.

Still terrified by the shame and guilt of failure, I took a deep breath, and revealed myself. I told them all about my affair, all about my husband reading my journals, everything. I ended my confession with, "I'm not perfect, Louise."

With her hands on my shoulders, looking deeply into my eyes, Louise brought me in very close to her and said, "Darling... did you really think I thought you were the only person who was?"

And you know what? I kind of did.

I know it sounds irrational. If I'd stopped to really

think about it, I would have realized that what I expected of myself was unrealistic. But I was operating on automatic pilot, and I was attached to the belief that I could somehow do it all without anyone ever seeing my weaknesses. Somewhere deep in my psyche was the belief that if they saw a weakness in me, everything would fall apart.

So I never asked for help. To me, asking for help would mean I wasn't enough. That I was a failure, imperfect. I couldn't have been more wrong.

The moment I felt Louise accept me—all of me—I started thinking of her as my personal "affirmation action figure." She saw me in a way that I had never been willing to see myself—as a human being with both strengths and weaknesses. She inspired me to embark on a path of self-discovery and self-love, and she gave me the courage to be transparent.

I wasn't perfect. I needed help. And that was okay.

This lesson was really solidified for me when, uncharacteristically, I found myself feeling ill off and on for a period of a year. It wasn't just your run of the mill cold or flu. I was dealing with adrenal fatigue and even had a serious bout with vertigo that made me dizzy, nauseated, lethargic, and gave me distorted, blurred vision.

I had never experienced anything like it. For ten days, I was completely ungrounded and housebound. Of course, I called Louise and asked, "What is going on?"

"This is the universe proving to you that you actually are not in control of anything and that you need to rest and surrender and receive," she told me.

The heart can hurt, the mind can deal, the emotions can get sorted out, but the body can take you out at the knees. I was essentially incapacitated, so I had no choice but to ask for help.

Through all of this, I learned the wisdom of my friend Wayne Dyer's words: "We are Divine enough to ask, and we are important enough to receive." Mindfulness meditation teacher Jon Kabat-Zinn puts it this way: "It is useful at times to admit to yourself that you don't know your way and to be open to help from unexpected places."

Receiving is Also Giving

When you make a big change in your life—when you *jump*—you need support. If you're a giver like me, you probably find it difficult to ask others to assist you. But think for a moment about how good it feels when you give to others. By not allowing someone else to give to *you*, you deprive them of that good feeling. So, when you receive, you're still giving. It's a win-win!

We hear all the time how it's better to give than to receive; how we need to be more giving; how wonderful it is to give. And it certainly is. But for the codependent among us, there is an imbalance to our giving. We offer much more than we get back, which isn't healthy. So learn to allow other people the pleasure of helping you.

When I asked some of my coaching clients to share their stories with me for the book, a part of me felt bad about it. They would have to go to the trouble of writing it out! Would they have time? Would they find it painful? Would it be a bother? But one after another thanked me for asking them. They learned something from writing it down. It was cathartic. It was helpful to them. It gave them pleasure to share their stories with you. Once again, I learned the value of asking for help—not just for my benefit as the recipient, but for the benefit of the givers as well.

Here's another example. I've known finance guru Suze Orman for years, but when my divorce left me worrying about some outstanding financial issues, I hesitated to ask my friend for advice. I didn't want to impose on her, thinking that people must do that all the time, and it must make her crazy. But one day while we were on tour in Australia, I got up the courage to ask this Emmy-winning, *New York Times* bestselling powerhouse what I should do about a specific situation.

Suze is honestly one of the most loving and spiritual people I know, and while she certainly couldn't possibly help all of the people who approach her, she told me that it was her service and pleasure to help her friends. After all, Suze's motto is "People first. Then money. Then things." Besides the great financial advice she gave me that day, she also taught me that asking for help allows us to honor the gifts and talents of someone else and gives that person a chance to shine, doing what they do best.

So, if you still think it's selfish to receive, realize that you're actually not allowing someone else to have the pleasure of giving. Imagine a world where everyone feels it's too selfish to receive. No one would have that profound pleasure of knowing they've helped someone else. Know that the world functions in a healthier way with a balanced, steady flow back and forth.

Poet and novelist Lawrence Learner said, "The difference between a helping hand and an outstretched palm is a twist of the wrist." In her poem, "To Begin With, the Sweet Grass," Mary Oliver put it like this: "It's giving until the giving feels like receiving."

Don't Get Lost in the Details

Close friends can offer you emotional support as you move through your transition, and all sorts of people can help you with the logistics of your jump. In my case, divorce involved a range of legal issues—dividing up property, finances, etc. It all seemed far too technical for me. Where does one even begin? I used logistics as an excuse to postpone my decision, using my feelings of helplessness as an excuse. I didn't know *how* to get divorced, so how could I? I remember feeling so hopeless about how we would divide up our book collection that I decided divorce was not an option. It wasn't until I was desperate that I finally asked people who understood divorce for help.

There's also this thing called the "internet." So you don't even have to ask a real, live *person*. If you're willing to seek help, I promise you'll find people (live or online) to help you with all the details. When I allowed others to help me, I suddenly felt less alone. I also got other perspectives based on a wider range of knowledge.

There's a little story I love that expresses this better than I could:

A little boy was having difficulty lifting a heavy stone. His father came along just then. Noting the boy's failure, he asked, "Are you using all your strength?"

"Yes, I am," the little boy said impatiently.

"No, you are not," the father answered. "I am right here just waiting, and you haven't asked me to help you."

GOOD STORY.

Vulnerability is Beautiful

One of the reasons I refused to ask for help for so long

was that I didn't want to appear vulnerable. I'd spent a long time thinking that "strength" meant being totally invulnerable. Never letting them see me sweat, as I've said. But it turns out that it takes *way* more courage to say "I don't know how to do this" and "I can't do it alone."

It felt scary to let anyone see what I judged as my "weaknesses," but as it turned out, it was safer than I realized. As soon as I asked for help, I discovered how many people were not only willing but were *happy* to give me whatever I needed.

Showing my vulnerability made me appear more human to others. I had projected the image of "superwoman," and they had actually believed me! Once I let down my shield, they could identify with me and relate to me for the first time. The result was that they felt closer to me. They were all human, too, and they had all felt vulnerable.

I also discovered that asking for help ends loneliness. I slowly started allowing people more into my world so that they could see all of me—both my "efficient" self and the part of me who throws up her hands and says, "I don't know." Feeling "help-*less*" wasn't necessary anymore, though, because help was always right there. I only had to ask.

Jen Tells Her Story

Doubt. Insecurity. Questions surrounding my capabilities in my mind; traveling in circles like a wind-up doll. I wondered, "Why does it come so easily to others but not to me?"

I remember sitting in my high school classes, looking at the teachers as if they were speaking another language and glancing at peers for their guidance and their papers for the answers. I was lost and not seen. I kept thinking, "If only someone would just open their eyes, glance over and really see me."

I was the student who needed to be looked at through a different lens. I wanted to learn but not much was sticking. Somehow, I got by. Middle school, high school and then college. College was when it hit me.

Ironically, I began dating a guy from Harvard. Each time I visited the campus I had to listen to this running dialogue in my mind: "You are going to be okay." "They will love you for who you are, not because of what you don't know." "They will see the beauty within; trust yourself." It was helpful at times, but exhausting overall.

I am a dancer. I studied all throughout my education and continue to this day. I believe that through my dancing, I was able to find the confidence I needed to start the process of self-acceptance.

Barbara was a therapist. She was empathetic, understanding, and insightful. Within two sessions, she sent me to meet Katie, an educator. She was not your typical professor. Katie had many degrees that all meshed together to create one of the most intuitive people I had ever met. The first two sessions were filled with evaluations. After they were completed, she asked, "Have you ever heard of Howard Gardner?" I said no. She explained to me that Howard wrote a book called *Frames of Mind*, which describes his theory of multiple intelligences. He defines intelligence in many ways, one of which is called bodily-kinesthetic.

People who have bodily-kinesthetic intelligence learn better by involving muscular movement (moving around into the learning experience). Katie explained that I have a high level of kinesthetic intelligence. She told me that I learn best with visuals. Conversation about issues, mathematics, and science helps me hold on to the information more. She began breaking big ideas down into smaller groups. I was having success.

Along with seeing Katie for three years, I continued to see Barbara for two of those three years. The combination of Katie's compassion and education alongside Barbara's empathy and insight allowed the deep discovery of my true confidence to be found. The mental and emotional expansion was exhilarating.

Not only did I feel that I had a handle on life, but I also knew how to break things down for the future. I had tools that would stay with me throughout my lifetime. The best thing that came out of this work was gaining a deep understanding of who I am. First, I learned to be patient with myself instead of critical. I learned to appreciate instead of looking for more. I let go of any false expectations and began to see the power in my contribution. I embraced it and gave myself credit for what I was good at.

I was validated and proud of what I had to offer. This work with Barbara and Katie eventually led me to find my calling—working with National Dance Institute, transforming the lives of tens of thousands of New York City public school children and their communities through weekly classes, short-term residencies, and public performances. And all from being willing to ask for help.

Help With Learning How to Ask For Help

1. If you find it difficult to ask for help, ask yourself this question: What do I think will happen if I ask someone to support me emotionally or provide some other type of assistance that I need?

2. Chances are, the fears you have about asking for help are irrational. Fear might tell you, for example, that the people you ask will feel put-upon or will say no to you. So, let's take this exercise a step further. What would happen if someone said no to your request? Can you survive the feelings of rejection and ask someone else? Even if one or two people are unwilling to help you, there are probably others in your life willing to help. And if there aren't, it's time to cultivate some new friendships that are more nourishing for you—friends who value you and who are willing to have a healthy give and take in your relationship.

3. Mary Catherine Bateson, who is a writer, anthropologist, and the daughter of Margaret Mead,

says: "The reality of all life is interdependence. We need to compose our lives in such a way that we both give and receive, learning to do both with grace, seeing both as parts of a single pattern rather than as antithetical alternatives." Visualize yourself living a life of balance between giving and receiving. Imagine yourself receiving help and love from the people you care about most. Write down how it feels. Does it feel great or uncomfortable? Do you feel selfish? If there is discomfort, describe that feeling. What worries you about it? Do you feel you don't deserve it? Do you worry that there will be a backlash or that you will "owe" these people something in return that you fear you cannot give? What would it feel like to receive without a price tag attached to it? What if someone said, "I'm going to give this to you, and you owe me nothing in return"?

4. Think about when you give to others. Are you able to give to them without feeling that they must return the favor? The next time you give to someone, work on letting go of the price tag. If you can give unconditionally, you can then begin to receive unconditionally.

5. Imagine receiving advice from the person you admire the most. What would this person say to you?

6. Identify five different things you need right now in order to feel supported. Now identify five people in your life you can ask for that support.

7. Get out your phone. I mean it! Right this minute, I want you to text, call, or email three of the five

people you listed, and ask them for the support you need. Think of it as a research project if nothing else. Will the sky really fall if they say no? What if they say yes?

A MOMENT TO FORGIVE

If, like me, you tend to give more than you let yourself receive, there may be resentment hiding out in your psyche. You may be somewhat spent by all that you have given, getting so little in return. The world is constantly offering us opportunities to receive. The trick is to open yourself up to receiving more. You must be willing.

In order to allow in more of what you need and want, first forgive yourself for taking better care of others than you have taken of yourself. Your intentions were good and loving.

Then forgive others for taking from you, sometimes perhaps in a selfish way. You allowed it. And starting right now, you can change that story. You can allow more of a balance—a flow—of giving and receiving in your life. It doesn't mean you'll find that balance in every moment, but you'll make decisions about giving and asking for help from a place of heightened awareness.

Step Seven
Honor Your Resistance

I sat on my couch staring out my big picture window toward Boulder Creek feeling furious and frustrated. I was waiting for my husband to sign our divorce papers. "Why is it taking him so long?" I thought. "I wish he'd hurry up and get it over with."

Two seconds later, I found myself fantasizing about him breaking down the door to our apartment and riding in like a knight on a horse to get me and work it out.

What? *I wanted this divorce!* Why was I still imagining him coming back? I thought I was going a bit crazy. Over time, I've come to realize that it's natural to feel ambivalent about important life decisions. The truth is that I had resistance to staying married ... *and* resistance to getting divorced. I love a line in Elizabeth Gilbert's book *Eat, Pray, Love:* "The only thing more unthinkable than leaving was staying; the only thing more impossible than staying was leaving." Yep, that was me.

This kind of inner conflict is one of the ways we stay stuck. As long as we're sitting on the fence, we don't have to pick a side, hop down, and get on with our lives. Since this book is one massive attempt to help you disengage from your inner stalemate and make the best decision you can, we've got to talk about resistance.

You *will* have doubts. It's not a one-time deal; you will inevitably have to make your choice over and over. I had to keep choosing to get divorced and not go back ...

over and over again. I had to reevaluate my decision more times than I can count. In fact, it became a daily practice.

None of us likes change. Our natural impulse is to come up with all sorts of reasons why we should stay right where we are. So, around this time in the Jump process, you can expect your mind to start making a case (if it hasn't already) for why change is impossible and why you shouldn't do it. You'll have to keep reminding yourself what you want and why the change *is* necessary … in spite of your resistance. And, yes, you'll have to keep choosing, every day and every moment, to move forward—toward your more positive future.

Emmanuel, as channeled by the late Pat Rodegast, once said, "We all work with an enormous collection of fear voices telling us why we must not be who we are." When you make a big change in your life (sometimes even when you make a small change), those voices get louder. They're trying desperately to pull you back into what they believe is safety. But remember that this fear is irrational; it's a retreat from life. Plus, it doesn't actually help you avoid pain. It does, however, prevent you from experiencing as much joy and excitement and growth in your life as you could.

You may never be able to silence those voices, but you can learn to pay less attention to them. You can say, "Thank you very much for sharing" and continue on with courage. Dr. Christiane Northrup says, "We heal through repetition. Each time on the spiral we go back to the same place but we're on a higher rung, or deeper section of that particular issue." So, every time you act in spite of your fear voices, you grow stronger.

We heal through repetition

The most important thing to remember about your resistance is that it isn't necessarily a sign you should abandon your plan to jump. There were many times when I thought it would be easier to just go back to my husband because it was my comfort zone. It was the known. Of course, the *un*known is very *un*comfortable. But it wouldn't have been easier at all to stay in my marriage. By then I had seen too much of what I wanted and who I was meant to be. I couldn't go back.

For me, leaving my husband felt like committing identity suicide. I had to become a new person in many respects, living my life on my own terms and not putting someone else's needs before my own. I had to learn to think for myself and not be dependent on someone else's opinion to confirm my own. I had to learn how to go on stage and allow the real, imperfect me to be seen without the mask that I had protected for so long.

Ultimately, there would be a B.D. me—Before Divorce—and an A.D. me—After Divorce. The new me would *never* have remained in the marriage I had before. There would be no room for the A.D. me in that marriage. He needed a woman I wasn't anymore, and the new me would have needed a man he never was. So, going back wasn't an option, no matter what my resistance tried to tell me.

At first I thought I had to "muscle" through my resistance—endure it or outlast it. But that doesn't work. It was only once I acknowledged, embraced, and honored the wisdom inherent in my resistance that it began to ease. At that point, I could feel nostalgic without going back. I could recognize that the sensations of fight or flight were just the past knocking, and I didn't have to answer that knock. I could simply become comfortable with the resistance and make the choice to jump anyway.

Resistance is like a beach ball. When you push it underwater, it pops back up to the surface even stronger. (Thanks to wise author and dear friend Debbie Ford for that great analogy.) So, as you move closer to making your jump, accept that resistance is bound to pop up to the surface and maybe even hit you in the face. Don't push it back down. Let it be there. Rather than caving in to it or running away from it, try honoring it. Invite it in for tea. Make friends with it. Ask it what it has to say. Then, no matter how loud it screams, remind yourself that you don't have to give in to its demands. It's just part of the process.

Besides your own resistance, of course, you might encounter resistance from other people in your life. Poet e.e. cummings said, "To be nobody but yourself, in a world which is doing its best to make you everybody else, means to fight the hardest battle which any human being can fight, and never stop fighting." As you reinvent yourself, some people in your life will be attached to their image of who you are. Don't let them turn you into someone you are not. It isn't worth it!

Remember what that other very wise poet David Whyte said about someone inevitably feeling betrayed when we live the life we are meant to live. That was certainly true in my case. It was important for me to keep moving in the direction that was right for me and to communicate my position firmly to others as necessary. But the reality is that resistance will present itself in various forms.

Melinda Tells Her Story

When I was set to leave my husband, I just couldn't find the strength in myself to do it. It was like wanting to jump in the cold creek, fearing it, and making my resistance dance on the rock. I knew I would jump, but oh, God, not yet!

Then a friend said, "It's not going to hurt any less tomorrow, is it?"

My whole body and soul were burning. Years and years of safety, albeit not what I wanted, were pressing on me, pulling me back to what was familiar. But somehow the determination to stay true to myself took over. I knew that after the first shock, that creek was going to feel so good. I knew I would feel so alive and thankful if I jumped in.

So, I did! And, yes, I did feel alive and so very thankful.

Is It Resistance or Wisdom?

How do you know if what you're feeling is just resistance and not a sign that jumping would be a mistake? How do you know if it's an excuse in logical clothing or a warning sign that you don't want to ignore?

If you feel *defensive* about making a change, if you're making excuses for why you *can't* make the change, or if you feel defeated before you even begin, you are probably experiencing resistance. If you want the change but feel you can't let go of what you already have, you are probably experiencing resistance. If you're trying to convince yourself that your current life isn't so bad, you're experiencing resistance.

Emmanuel said, "Set aside who you are supposed to be and become who you really are, and be willing to savor that experience. In the beginning, it may be hard to tell if you are really being who you are, but eventually—and this is a promise—your heart will sing and you will have touched the essence of your being. Once you have touched it, you can never more pretend you do not know the essence of love that you are."

The antidote to excuses is taking responsibility and making choices. Reconnect with what you want. When you envision your life after the change, how does it feel? Do you feel excited by the possibilities? Imagine what it would be like to let go of fear and have whatever you want. If there were no consequences whatsoever, which choice would you make—to stay the same or to change?

> *When we stop resisting and surrender to the situation exactly as it is, things begin to change.*
> —Debbie Ford

Surrender and Release

Resistance creates a dam, a self-imposed barrier that prevents the new from coming into your life. As you honor your resistance, the dam comes down, and the waters of change begin to flow. But any attempt to push the experience away—to resist the resistance—creates another dam. It's complicated! Which is part of the reason that big change doesn't happen overnight.

We let go of the past a little bit at a time, so it may take a while to surrender. For a long time, I continued to feel emotionally triggered whenever my husband tried to contact me or when his name was mentioned. One day, sometime after the divorce, I was in a hotel lobby in Melbourne, Australia, with Louise Hay when I got a text from my ex. I proceeded to have an emotional meltdown in Louise's arms. She looked at me and said, "You will continue to be tested until you are no longer triggered."

Luckily, the tests are far fewer today. I'm not saying I'm emotionally dead around the situation at this point, but I'm no longer tempted to go backwards. That's what I mean by surrendering to the new. You let yourself get drawn into the gravitational pull of a positive future so much that there is no longer a risk of falling back into old patterns and habits.

Even if it takes a long time, eventually you'll get to a place of surrender—and the past will release its grip on you. It's a wonderful feeling; it's something you can look forward to. In the meantime, however, you must make the choice to jump because jumping is what facilitates the process.

Stop Resisting Your Resistance

1. Allow yourself to throw an "I don't want to jump!" tantrum, while also holding the space for a wonderful miracle when you do make that jump. Experience the opposing feelings without trying to resolve the paradox.

2. Do another excuse inventory, writing down all of the obstacles in your way. These could be your own feelings, the feelings of others, physical logistics, etc. Exhaust all of the reasons your mind tells you that you can't and shouldn't jump. Now burn your excuse inventory.

3. Visualize a door with a pinhole. On the other side of that door is the future you want—the other side of your jump. Look through that pinhole and see that future. Allow the pinhole to get bigger and bigger so that the view of this new life becomes clearer and clearer. Write down what you see. If you can, imagine the door popping open. Can you walk through?

4. Write down ten good reasons to make the jump— ten things that will be possible for you when you let go of your excuses and go for it—when you walk through that door into your future.

Are You Ready to Jump?

Teacher and author Caroline Myss says, "If you're getting directions, 'Move on with your life, let go of something,' then do it. Have the courage to do it. This is the way it is. When you get guidance to let go of something, it's sort of like a time warning that says, 'You have ten days left. After that, your angel's going to do it.' So, the desire to hold on is not going to stop the process of change."

The trick is to honor the resistance and jump anyway.

A MOMENT TO FORGIVE

Take a moment now to forgive yourself for resisting what is good for you. Forgive yourself for staying in a situation that doesn't serve you. Forgive yourself for resisting your birthright to pleasure, joy, and love, and commit to opening your heart and your life to that birthright. You have a whole new future ahead of you!

Step Eight
Jump!

I was once again in a hotel with Louise Hay. (You are getting a true picture of what my life is like!) This time I was lamenting the fact that I *wanted* to jump, but felt too afraid. Big-time resistance!

"It's like wanting to get to the other side of the river, yet clinging to a branch on this side for dear life," Louise told me. "The only way we can possibly land over there is to release our grip."

Lulu, as she is affectionately known, was absolutely right of course. For a long time, I'd tried to have it both ways. I was stretched all the way across that river, not letting go of the past and not fully embracing my future. But there comes a time when we have to trust our own ability to swim, even if we can't see the other side. We have to trust that we *can* power ourselves to the other side, and that land will be there to greet us.

Jumping is not only about letting go and leaving, but also about propelling ourselves toward the new—even when we don't know exactly what the "new" will be! I had no idea what would be coming my way when I left my marriage. I'd been with this man for eighteen years, after all, and we not only lived together but also worked together. Our lives were completely intertwined. Who would I be without him? I could hardly imagine who this A.D. ("After Divorce") me would be. It was like standing at the edge of a cliff so high that I couldn't see the river down below.

What I've since discovered is that we're constantly being pushed to the edge of that precipice, and the only thing to do is to muster enough faith to jump into the uncertainty. As writer Ray Bradbury said, "You've got to jump off cliffs all the time and build your wings on the way down."

I know how scary that sounds, trust me. But isn't it scarier to remain stuck in a life that you know for sure isn't working? That's certainly what I faced with my marriage. That life wasn't working, but I was so afraid to let it go that for years I wouldn't admit—not even to myself—how unhappy I truly was.

When my husband kicked me out of the house, and I finally did not go back, the ground beneath my feet was gone—literally. I was no longer living in my home. This was huge. I was already starting to become the "A.D." version of Nancy, as everything I'd known myself to be was annihilated. Remember that identity suicide I mentioned? Well, to my surprise, I was still here, and ground *did* appear beneath my feet. I actually wasn't that identity I thought was me. I was much, much more.

So are you. There is so much more to you than you realize. The person your mind thinks you are is only a fraction of your totality. We are not our identities. All of the labels you put on yourself, all of the concepts and beliefs you have about who you are actually serve to make you *smaller* than you truly are.

Stay Off the Brakes

When learning how to mountain bike I was taught to avoid grabbing the brakes while descending, even though there are rocks and branches in the way. The rule is: If you focus on the rock in front of you, you'll hit it. Instead, look ahead of you on the trail where you *want* to go. Grabbing the brakes stops the flow of the ride. It has been a hard lesson for me because the impulse is to brake the minute I see a rock in the way. I have to constantly remind myself to keep looking in the direction I'm heading.

The same is true in life, anytime we jump toward something new. Grabbing the brakes limits us. In the last step, we discussed honoring our resistance. As you do so, you put yourself into that all-important flow. As a result, you can keep your eyes on the future. Soon, with way less effort than you'd imagine, you'll be soaring toward it.

The Defining Moment

Yes, and for many of us, that moment is when we know we can't bear to stay in the old life a moment longer. As writer Anaïs Nin said, "And the day came when the risk to remain tight in a bud was more painful than the risk it took to blossom."

My hope is that the process in this book will bring you to your own moment—the moment when you'll know that the pain of staying is worse than the pain of jumping. There may be a "last straw" event, or it may be a subtle inner shift. Either way, you'll know.

If you still feel stuck and aren't sure whether to make

your jump, go back and review the previous seven steps. Do the exercises again, and see if new insights come to you.

If not, put the book aside for a week or two, and begin to notice the small changes that have already taken place in your life. Big change is often just a collection of small alterations. Take the time to look around you, as well as inside you, and notice how different things already are. These moments are rare in our lives—don't miss them! You can even ask a close friend if he or she has noticed changes in you. Then, go back to the steps and exercises again.

If you feel that no "defining moment" presents itself to you, simply take responsibility for choosing your own turning point. Don't forget, though, that doubts *will* come up—even after your defining moment. Remember that the habit will be to worry about the logistics and the "how" the change will happen. Our tendency is to try to figure things out, but there is more to be gained from the state of not knowing. Only in the uncertainty can something new emerge.

The so-called safety of certainty and knowing is overrated. Think about it: There is nothing new in what you already know. It's limited. There's a ceiling. *Not* knowing, on the other hand, is expansive. In the not knowing is where the unexpected comes, where possibility lives. I used to hate not knowing, but I've learned to let myself be within it (at least better than the B.D. me) and to trust that something good is coming my way. Don't let fear tell you that the new is always bad. In that place of not knowing, anything can unfold. And that's exciting, if you allow it to be.

DEFINING MOMENTS

What follows are three stories of defining moments that I hope will help you recognize your own when it arrives.

Daniel Tells His Story

Several years ago, after an intense and rather revealing session of bodywork, I realized that I was being smothered by the life I had created for myself. I did not feel smothered by life itself, but rather trapped by my own self-created identities. And no matter how hard I tried, I couldn't seem to escape it.

By that time, I had been working in prisons for fourteen years, and while that work had been some of the most rewarding work I had ever done, what I didn't realize was that I was using it as a place to hide out. I didn't want to admit my own discontent, restlessness, and longing, which are all signs that change is on the way. The life I had constructed for myself, for various reasons, had become, in a very real way, its own sort of prison.

My body was screaming, telling me that I needed to take drastic measures to break free of some very deeply entrenched patterns. It was painfully evident that I needed to initiate new cycles of change—not small changes, but major life changes. Knowing that the body is an intuitive system through which guidance enters my life I took heed. Everything around me and within me was telling me it was time for change and liberation.

At that moment, I invited sweeping change into my life. I remember, as if it were yesterday, declaring to God that I wanted the winds of change to blow through my life and reorganize everything. Every cell and atom in my body aligned with the energetic forces that animate me—my spirit, mind, heart, and will. And an intention was so clearly, so deliberately declared that I knew life would never be the same.

A door opened. Michael, my partner, was offered a job in Albuquerque, New Mexico. While I could easily come up with a list of at least five places I would be happy to move to, Albuquerque was definitely not one of them. And with all the places I've been in the world, I had never been to New Mexico.

All I could hear in my head was a voice saying, "You wanted drastic change, so here it is!" I have to tell you honestly that I was not crazy about Albuquerque, not at all. But I couldn't ignore the fact that the universe doesn't make mistakes, and I don't believe in coincidences. We had to make a choice. Did I have the guts to follow through? Was I crazy to leave a beautiful home in Hawaii, one of the most magical places on the planet? Was I insane to quit a job that I invested fourteen years in and which afforded me a good living? How would it feel to say "goodbye" to a lifetime of family and friends? Could I handle the high desert?

The voice of reason and logic stepped in. There was no logical reason to leave, and when all was said and done, it even appeared that it might be wise to remain in Hawaii. Then the voice of Caroline Myss echoed through my mind: "When making a choice, always choose what requires the most faith." Remaining in Hawaii required no faith whatsoever. We both knew we had to take a leap of faith and follow through with what our souls were communicating to us. It was time to let go and move forward. *Life is about expanding into the unknown and exploring the mysteries that surround us.*

Never in a million years did I think or imagine that I would be living in Albuquerque, New Mexico. But here I am, quite happy.

We're always being called to make different choices that will change the direction of our lives, choices that will force us to reevaluate who we are, relinquish relationships to people, places, and things, and also reestablish ourselves in new locations. We're called upon to make choices that will ignite new creative energies within and around us. I'll be the first to admit that it is scary, uncomfortable, and aggravatingly inconvenient sometimes. But it's also wildly invigorating, immensely liberating, and terrifically beneficial!

Rebecca Tells Her Story

For years, I realized that my automatic go-to reaction when I was frustrated or scared was to get angry. I used to think that was just how I was wired. But in May 2011 I was at a concert in the park with my husband, children, and friends. My daughter, who was eleven at the time, ran off with her friends. I couldn't find her at first and panicked. When I did find her, I was filled with anger and rage that she disobeyed my specific instructions to stay within eyesight.

I can remember grabbing her arm and yelling at her in front of everyone. What I didn't realize is that I had gotten so angry that my nails left a mark in her arm. I woke up the next morning in shock that I could get so angry and realized that I was carrying on a legacy of anger that, if not addressed, would be passed onto my daughter.

It was at that time that I returned to Debbie Ford's work and discovered the shadow of anger that had controlled so much of my life. It was as if this world of understanding opened up to me and provided me with the possibility of a new way of being and relating to people.

I can remember feeling scared when I started the work, but so elated when I discovered that I no longer had to be controlled by anger. Instead, I found the gifts in it! That moment and the subsequent work I did have truly altered my ability to see the world. But most of all, they have changed my relationship with my daughter!

Kate Tells Her Story

I had two choices: Do something to make a difference for myself and others or just live in fear of what might or might not happen.

Right after I was diagnosed with multiple sclerosis (MS), I was riding in the elevator to a doctor's appointment and overheard someone talking about a bike ride to benefit MS. Before I understood any of the details, I knew it was something I had to do. Oddly enough, I would not consider myself an impulsive person, but I was moved to do something that was so out of my comfort zone.

There are very few things I have been extremely passionate about in my life, but this became one of them. I registered for the ride before I even had a road bike or thought about fundraising, and I wasn't sure if I could actually finish the ride. I bought an awesome bike and started riding. Training for the ride became so much more than just training. I had never been comfortable asking for money, but when I began fundraising, money flowed in. I had no idea what to expect, and it was better than I ever could have imagined.

Here are my MS bike ride stats over the past six years (2008-2013): I rode 150 miles in 3 rides; rode 175 miles the other 3 rides; raised $147, 618.28; and have been the #2 fundraiser for five years in Northern California.

Time to Walk Toward the Precipice

Now, it's your turn to head toward the precipice. Remember to breathe!

1. You have already written about your resistance. Let's look at what has changed already for you as a result of this process—new feelings, new beliefs, new habits. Finish as many of the sentences that follow as you can.

Something new I believe is _____
Something new I feel is _____
Something new I understand is _____
One change I have experienced is _____
_____

I never expected to feel _____
I never expected to believe _____
I never expected to understand _____
_____

2. Write an invitation to the current you from the future you that says something like, "I invite you to the other side of the river. The water is fine." Continue the letter with the comforting words you need to make the jump. Allow this future you to write a description of your brighter future from the perspective of one year from now. Write it in the present tense, and describe the feelings, sensations, activities, experiences of being there. Have fun with it, and make it as vivid as you can.

Karen Tells Her Story

My big jump has been about being openly and unabashedly a lesbian. Growing up in the 1980s (when the social climate was not as welcoming as it is today, and the common wisdom was that it wasn't worth the risk to be honest) taught me a skill it has taken the rest of my life to unlearn. Back then, my biggest concern was how to navigate around uncomfortable conversations about my personal life that might give someone a clue that all was not as it seemed. Editing

---

my words instead of telling an outright lie used to seem like a convenient workaround that kept me from having to look at myself as a liar. Every story had two versions—the truth and the *real* truth.

Someone would ask: "What did you do on your vacation?"

I would answer: "I went to the beach in Mexico." True, except that I went with my girlfriend to celebrate our second anniversary.

I would say, "This is Marla. She lives here, too." True, except we slept together in the master bedroom, and that other bedroom that we pretended was hers was really where we sorted the laundry. In fact, we spent three hours dusting and vacuuming it to make it look like someone lived in there before my mother arrived for a visit.

It took me a long time to realize that what we allow people to believe is actually what we are presenting as truth. And the truth we present about ourselves determines a lot more than we know. In fact, the story we tell about ourselves can keep us from the very best connections in which people have the opportunity to see us as we really are and love us anyway.

Today, I believe that misleading with the intent to deceive is still lying.

So my girlfriend and I were both in graduate school, and we rented a two-bedroom apartment so that anyone who came to visit would assume that we each had our own rooms.

At the end of our lease, we realized that if we moved into a one-bedroom apartment, we would save enough money to be able to buy some new shoes once in a while and possibly even make our car payments regularly. That meant there would be no convenient way to lie about the fact that we slept in the same double bed, short of going the Rob-and-Laura-Petrie-twin-bed route.

This predicament was the source of many tearful and fearful conversations about the possibility of our families disowning us. We eventually decided that our ability to occasionally eat some protein depended upon it. So we did it.

Then one day her mother came to visit. In the hours before her arrival, I experienced a volume of flop sweat that I don't recall ever experiencing before or since. Marla's mom looked around the apartment, made some small talk with me, and didn't say a word about the bedroom. Not one.

As Marla and her mother left for lunch, my mind raced with all of the possibilities. Was she going to whisk Marla into an unmarked van and take her to a mental hospital? Would I come home one day to find Marla's dad waiting in the bushes, ready to introduce my head to a baseball bat? Those were some of the better outcomes I imagined in those couple of hours.

When I heard Marla's key in the door, I had worked myself into such a frenzy that I literally jumped over the dog and our crappy green couch with the harvest gold flowers that my aunt threw away, moving at warp speed to the door. But she was smiling.

"My mom said she wondered how long we were going to pretend we don't sleep together. She said she has felt so distant from me, and it has made her sad. She was afraid to ask me because she figured I wasn't ready to tell her, but she has felt really bad that I thought it was better to lie."

And that is when I realized that people are usually smarter than we give them credit for, and all the editing in the world doesn't hide the truth. It just makes us look like liars and denies us the gift of real connection.

Telling the rest of the world about how happy I am to be a lesbian is a cakewalk compared to letting Marla's mother see that double bed. That experience led to being open about who I am. No compromises, no hiding.

Commit to the Jump

Up until now, you have made unconscious commitments to fear and the comfort of the familiar. Now make a conscious commitment to the momentum of the decision you've made. Don't overthink it. It isn't about doing it right; it's just about doing it.

Enjoy the feeling of gravity as you go over the cliff's edge.

Jump.

Do it.

Now.

> *The door has opened, so there's no escape.*
> —Shams of Tabriz, an ancient Persian poet

A MOMENT TO FORGIVE

If you're still holding on and unable to jump, ask yourself what you need to forgive in order to make your jump. Is there some feeling of resentment that's holding you back—either toward yourself or someone else? Forgive and release any negativity that has a hold on you. Breathe it out and breathe in newness and freedom.

Step Nine
The Graceful Exit

When I was finally in the process of getting divorced, I didn't think it was about anything more than my marriage ending. Little did I know it would be the catalyst for my rebirth. Any major transition has the capacity to be such a catalyst. It's up to us to allow in what is possible—whether blissful or challenging—and respond to it in a life-affirming way.

Every entrance is also an exit. Journalist and speaker Ellen Goodman put it eloquently when she said, "There's a trick to the 'graceful exit.' It begins with the vision to recognize when a job, a life stage, or a relationship is over—and let it go. It means leaving what's over without denying its validity or its past importance to our lives. It involves a sense of future, a belief that every exit line is an entry, that we are moving up, rather than out."

Just as you honored your resistance, you must also honor where you've been. After you've jumped, it isn't like you never turn around and look back. You're human, and you're going to. You will still have doubts. In the "Honor Your Resistance" step, I said that you could jump before all of your resistance was resolved. This means that even *after* you jump, you will have to contend with those feelings. That's okay. It's all part of the graceful exit process.

So, just as you honored your resistance, it's important to honor what brought you to this moment. As I write this, it has been three years since my divorce mediation.

The person I am now would never have agreed to the terms I accepted in the settlement then. Ironically, however, I would never have become this A.D. me had I not experienced the anger I felt about the terms of our divorce. And of course if my husband had never read my journals at all—wow, my life would be very different today. Actually, it would have been the same as my B.D. life. I have no doubt that I would have stayed in my marriage. I wouldn't have written two books, I wouldn't have a coaching practice, and I wouldn't be sharing my story on stage before thousands to help others on a regular basis. That crisis opened the door to everything else that has happened since, and a lot of what has happened has been wonderful.

Wikipedia has a fascinating entry under the term "graceful exit." Apparently, this is the name of a computer program that "detects a serious error condition and 'exits gracefully' in a controlled manner as a result." Wikipedia goes on to say that "code for a graceful exit exists when the alternative—allowing the error to go undetected and unhandled—would produce serious errors or later anomalous behavior that would be more difficult for the programmer to debug." What a metaphor for the graceful exit after a jump in life!

The graceful exit program also requires that files be closed and sometimes a "core dump" must be performed. That leads me to a discussion of grief.

Surrender to Grief

I found that the graceful exit step involved diving deeply into the memories of my marriage. There was a lot of longing in that phase. So much reminded me of my past—the day a friend came over and made me dinner, for example, and the familiar aroma of roasting chicken and root vegetables unexpectedly brought back memories of my husband cooking for us in the kitchen. A deep grief enveloped me as a result. I was acutely aware of what I had lost—the promise I'd felt on my wedding day.

Rituals from our marriage would come back at unexpected moments. One that still lingers is the memory of taking off my ski boots just outside the door of our home in Telluride, Colorado, as our dogs feverishly licked my nose. Remembering that ritual after the jump, after leaving my marriage, and months (and years) after seeing my dogs for the last time, flooded me with the sensation of loss. The dogs became a symbol of my past. I was not just divorced; I was dogless.

Sometimes the emotions were overwhelming. The grief was confusing to me at first. I knew it wasn't about wanting to go back, but it was still intense. Soon I discovered that when I allowed those visceral reminders to be there, I could easily move through the emotions and emerge without fighting with them. When I fought, on the other hand, the feelings seemed to linger and fester. It took much more work to hold my painful emotions at bay than it did to let them flow. It was, in a way, a "core dump" of emotions.

Honoring your grief is akin to honoring your resistance, but there's a subtle difference: Grief is just a feeling; it isn't a setback. It's a passing visitor. Unlike resistance, which will do anything to keep you from moving forward, grief simply wants to be felt. Once again, its presence doesn't necessarily mean that you have chosen wrong. It doesn't mean you jumped prematurely or didn't jump far enough. No matter when you jump, you will have some grief. And sometimes, it will be intense.

But you can't let go of something that you haven't fully felt, so there's nothing to do but let the grief come. The only way you can truly say goodbye to anything is to allow everything you feel about it to be fully felt. This isn't the same as wallowing in your pain; it's about allowing your feelings to have their say. No graceful exit can happen until you accept what has been.

There's a fine line between memory and baggage, however. You do have to eventually let go of whatever you've been holding onto. This doesn't mean you won't still occasionally have painful memories. But if those memories keep you from fully inhabiting your new life, go back through the steps. Do one thing different, ask for help, imagine yourself free...

Melinda Tells Her Story

After my heartbreak, I had to learn at some point that it isn't all pain and that moments of joy and happiness are not a betrayal to my grieving process. I learned to savor the bittersweet moments of pain and joy together. The most essential part of this process has been cultivating and nurturing the intimacy of the conversation with myself, learning and finding the kindness and acceptance of myself just as I am in the moment. I tell myself, "For now, this is my best, and my best is good enough." Being heartbroken gave me the opportunity to feel again, find myself again, and every day, little by little, fall in love with myself.

What you embrace you can release,
and what you release,
with loving gratitude, creates space for
greater blessings in your life.
—Author and spiritual teacher Jennifer Hoffman

Growing Pains

Not everything will be roses and sunshine right after you jump. While after my jump my life transformed in amazing ways, as I've mentioned, there were still growing pains. The jump is only the beginning of your new life, and there's still work to do. It's natural to feel disoriented during this time or even a bit out of control.

This graceful exit period is the time when you have to deal with the logistics of your new life. You have to "implement" your new plan. So, if you haven't yet asked for help, do so now. For me, as I said, I had to get an attorney and other people who knew how to do this divorce thing. They helped me figure out how to move out of my house, get the paperwork done, divide up our stuff, etc., etc.—those nasty, often *not* fun logistics.

If you buy a new house, for example, you still have to arrange all of your stuff in the rooms. You have to get used to where everything is and create a new routine. You have to make your house a home.

Even through this transition period, you'll probably love your new house. When I started getting accustomed to being single again, I found that there were many things I loved about my divorce—like going to sleep alone, waking up alone, traveling alone, and doing what I wanted when I wanted without having to ask anyone else's preference. It was a luxury!

The new you is, in a sense, a new house. If you've committed identity suicide, as I did, you're relearning who you are in your essence. *You* will need to get used to the new you! The authentic self will come through when you're no longer performing, pretending, or denying—when you are true to yourself. Being authentic is a moment to moment proposition, of course. It's a never-ending journey.

The people in your life will have to get used to this new you as well. While I became accustomed to the "A.D." me, other people still related to me as if I was the "B.D." me. They still expected me to answer the phone at 3:00 a.m. for work, for example. I had to start training people to stop having those expectations.

I finally understood that I could teach people how to treat me. That was uncomfortable, but the rewards were well worth the discomfort. Eventually, most people adjusted to who I became and am still becoming. So be patient with the people in your life, just as you are patient with your own unfolding.

Kris Tells Her Story

When my husband left our marriage, it felt like I had to jump off a cliff by default when I wasn't ready and didn't want to. It wasn't until I was free-falling that my choice to survive and thrive kicked in. I had endured so much grief in my life that the next logical step seemed to be to either take myself out or rise like a Phoenix from the ashes. It was a crossroads I'm humbled by because I know that a lot of people suffering don't choose life. This is why I've found purpose from my pain by giving back to others.

The past two years have been the most harrowing and liberating experience I've endured in my life. Throughout the journey, I've longed for the comfort of my old life, but know in my heart I didn't walk through the fire of suffering to play small on the other side of a new one.

The following two commitments drive me to live beyond grief:

1. To bring more light to those suffering in darkness and despair by delivering hope and inspiration.

2. To be an example of resilience and forgiveness for my daughter.

Kris Adams : www.frenchwomancamping.com

Integrate the Past, the Now, and the Future

The graceful exit step is a transitional, "liminal" period. A liminal space is the space on either side of a boundary or threshold. You've detached from the old life, crossed the threshold into your new world, but you haven't yet fully integrated into the new life. It's a period of time that may feel like a void, but it allows you to integrate. You begin to adjust to all that has happened to you, everything you have experienced, and what you want.

I like what author Sheryl Paul has to say about transitions: "We habitually think of transitions as 'hard' or 'negative,' but what most people fail to recognize is that embedded in these predictable life-cycle occurrences are opportunities that invite us to spiral into our fears and grief so that we heal at deeper levels each time. Instead of powering through transitions as quickly as possible, we would benefit greatly by embracing them as the gifts that they are."

The work of integration—of entering, exiting, and jumping again and again into the new—is simply part of life. In the next step, I'll talk about finding joy in all of it!

Amy Tells Her Story

Something that has helped me let go of the fear that cripples me is learning to live in the grey rather than the black or the white. By that, I mean learning to accept that I won't know the outcome until I take the next step. That is really scary for me. I like a plan! I want to know exactly how it will all pan out, and when I step into the uncertainty, I get scared and want to abandon ship.

But learning that possibility is in the uncertainty has helped me. I just need to do the next thing, and the next step in the road will show itself. I have learned to be patient and take one step at a time. I have learned to lean into the grey. I have learned to cherish that space of not knowing, where everything is possible.

Living by a plan can be really boring (who knew?). Instead, living in the grey has spilled over into many areas of my life. I'm more tolerant, less judgmental, more excited. I find myself open to more "left field" opportunities, and opportunity really is all around! The grey has turned out to be the spark I always thought was missing.

Your Jump—Before and After

1. Building on the exercise you did in the last step about what you have grown to understand, feel, and believe, let's compare the old you with the new you. This will help you further recognize the changes that have already taken place inside you.

   The old me would do _____,
   and the new me does _____.
   The old me would _____,
   which the new me would never do.
   Instead, the new me would _____
   _____.
   If the old me hadn't experienced _____
   _____, the new me
   wouldn't know _____.

2. Journal everything you're feeling—the grief, heartbreak, depression, joy—the full range of emotions in this transition period. But as you do, always stay focused on the fact that you are in this place of graceful exiting/entering. You are not looking back to get caught in the net of the past.

A MOMENT TO FORGIVE

Forgive yourself for feeling uncomfortable with transitions, for expecting completion, and for fearing your grief.

   Forgive others for expecting you to be the old you and for having difficulty accepting the changes you have made in yourself.

Step Ten
Say Yes … And Then Say It Again … And Again

I had no idea my divorce would become the gateway to growth, bearing gifts of unforeseen opportunity. How could I know that I would become a coach, write books, and speak at Hay House events?

The same was true for Louise. She has said, "If I had stayed married, I would never have become Louise Hay. I would never have fulfilled my destiny. I had to be released."

I know exactly what Lulu means. Leaving my marriage was the hardest thing I've ever done, but as I've said, I survived it and actually thrived because of it. I love the new life that I've created. Besides the changes in my work, I now also understand the importance of telling the truth in the moment instead of letting things fester. I'm able to give and receive feedback with less fear that everything is personal. I'm better able to ask for help and accept what is given, and I'm freer than I've ever been.

Crazy as it sounds, I am so grateful that my husband read those journals. I didn't just get divorced; I rebuilt my relationship with myself, reclaimed my dreams, and discovered new ones. I firmly believe that the many opportunities that came my way would not have happened if I had stayed in the marriage.

How strange that the nature of life is change,
yet the nature of human beings is to resist change.
And how ironic that the difficult times we
fear might ruin us are the very ones
that can break us open and help us blossom
into who we were meant to be.
—Elizabeth Lesser, teacher and author of
Broken Open: How Difficult Times Can Help Us Grow

Learning to Say Yes

A pivotal moment for me came when two of my coworkers at Hay House asked me to write a poem for their wedding and read it at the ceremony. Reid Tracy was there, and he said, "Oh, you're a *real* poet!" Now, I had a master's degree in poetry writing, but it took Reid saying that to me before I truly believed it. I thought Reid hated poetry, but he asked me to start reading my poems before the keynote speakers at our conferences. It was the first of many yeses that I would say, even though I was scared out of my mind.

People came to the conferences to hear Louise Hay and Wayne Dyer, but a number of them told me afterward, "I thought I was here to listen to the speakers, but I realize I was sent here to listen to that poem." It shocked me.

For years, people had periodically asked me, "When are you going to be a speaker at the conferences?" I always answered, "Me? No, that's not my thing. I'm a producer, an emcee, not a teacher."

But after I had read my poems on stage for a while, Reid said, "Why don't you share some of your personal story, too?" That led to my becoming a speaker on the

Hay House circuit. Then he suggested I write a book of poems and, later, this book.

None of these experiences had even been in my realm of desires. I could never have imagined what would happen on the other side of my greatest fear. And it all came about from making the jump and saying yes, again and again. I said yes to getting on stage, telling my story, letting down my guard, falling in love again, not knowing, and much more. It was a jump without a mask or a cape.

So often, we automatically say no to new experiences. We don't already know what those experiences will be like, so we fear them. But how boring would it be if we already knew what every experience would be like? What if you'd known what your first kiss would feel like or the birth of your first child? There would be no magic or wonder in the world.

Again, knowing is limiting. It's the unknown where the mystery of life resides. The unknown holds what we wish for, because we all wish for something different. So don't push away the unknowns. Step into the joy, richness, and yumminess of life. As the ancient Sufi poet Rumi wrote, "Respond to every call that excites your spirit."

We have learned to automatically anticipate the worst, but there is so much wonder on the other side of the river if you let go of that branch. I'm a testament to that, as are so many of my coaching clients. Emmanuel said, "It is harder to say 'yes' to the wonder of life than to the pain and suffering because the world holds the superstition that it's far safer and more sane to be miserable than to be joyous. That is how we keep illusion alive. You are the first in line for any miracle that you want to bring, and do you dare to allow the empowerment that is your birthright to bring forth the miracle?".

Believe that you can bring opportunities into your life that will bring you joy, peace, adventure, and excitement. Emmanuel also said, "You are already soaring when you can at any given moment say, 'I wonder what will happen next!' That genuine curiosity surpasses fear."

Bonnie Tells Her Story

My thirtieth birthday kicked off with a surprise trip to Iceland. My husband had planned it all, even down to buying me thermals to shield me from the cold and a new bikini to wear in the geothermal pools. Life was good. Then the fun, safe, and secure bubble I was living in burst without warning. My father's health deteriorated, and he announced that he had stage 4 colon cancer. Seeing my robust father so weak and frail was agonizing, and watching my hero leave the earth was heart-wrenching. I didn't know if I would ever stop crying.

My husband, Arthur, was my rock during that time. He held me as I cried myself to sleep every night. He helped me breathe through one panic attack after the other. He was loving and comforting.

Then, less than three months after my dad passed, Arthur was killed instantly in a motorcycle accident.

It was then that I realized I had a choice. I could continue to cry and simply lie down and die, or I could keep going.

I chose to keep going.

It wasn't easy, but it was certainly worth it. As I moved through the grief, I discovered new opportunities and uncovered a whole new world. I did things I never before thought possible.

I ran a marathon. I became a certified chef. I started over … and over again, continuing to say yes to life.

I fell in love again. I got remarried. (I proposed!) I became a soul coach®. I wrote a book. I got my own radio show.

Healing takes courage. Hope takes action. Life is waiting for you to answer. My advice is: Keep going.

Yes, Yes, Yes

Here's another story from my own life about saying yes … and I mean *yes!* (Get ready, because this one is a doozy!) I was sitting across the table from my dear friend Kelly at our favorite restaurant in Boulder, The Kitchen, when she said two words that I had no idea were about to change my life: Orgasmic Meditation.

Yep, you read that right. *Orgasmic Meditation.*

She was telling me about the book project she was working on. She was helping a woman named Nicole Daedone write her new book, *Slow Sex: The Art and Craft of the Female Orgasm.* When I asked Kelly what "slow sex" meant, she told me the book was about a practice called OM or Orgasmic Meditation. OM— pronounced "om"—was apparently a practice where a woman (ahem) takes off her pants, lies down, and a fully clothed man strokes her genitals in a very particular way for fifteen minutes. Both participants keep their attention on the sensation they feel at the point of contact between them. After the fifteen minutes, each shares a moment of sensation they remember feeling during the OM, and then they get up and go about their days.

Seriously? But it got even more outrageous, because Kelly—my good friend, a totally normal person as far as I was concerned—was telling me that after working on the book and hearing about the practice for months, she herself wanted to try OMing.

As you might imagine, my eyes were as wide as saucers. I could barely wrap my brain around the practice, much less the fact that Kelly wanted to try it. She was not in a relationship, so she'd be OMing with a friend rather than a partner. I was surprised, quizzical, and intrigued. I have to admit that I wanted to know what this OM thing was all about.

I knew the organization that taught OM, OneTaste, was based in San Francisco. It just so happened that I was producing a conference there a couple of weeks later that I thought Kelly might want to attend. I invited her to come to the conference and use it as an excuse to try OM while she was in San Francisco.

"Oh my God, this is insane! I can't believe it," I said to her the day of the conference, as she left the venue for her lunch break—a.k.a. her first OM. "I want to hear everything!"

When she walked back into the conference just over an hour later, I could see that she was changed. Her cheeks were flushed; she was *glowing*. She said it had been simultaneously the weirdest and most embodying experience she had ever had. And she was going back the next day. I spent the entire weekend living vicariously through her juicy exploration.

A month later, Kelly had moved to San Francisco

to finish the book project and live in the OneTaste community, and I was inexplicably drawn to try the practice of OM myself. I was back in San Francisco, staying at my sister's house. I told my sister I was heading out to see a potential new author—I mean, how does one talk about this kind of thing? "Oh, I'm going across town to take off my pants, lie down, and get stroked. See you at 5:00!" I wasn't even entirely sure I knew what I was signing up for. But I trusted Kelly, and I could see how much of an impact it was having on her life. I met her at the apartment where she was staying, and we walked over to OneTaste together.

I sat in a tiny room with two OM coaches, trying to relax and breathe normally. They asked me about my current and historic relationship to sex, desire, and pleasure. I explained that I was just a few months separated from my ex-husband and that I believed I had been born without a libido. Sex had always been just one more item on my endless "to do" list—something to do just for *him*. Suddenly, though, as part of my own self-inquiry and part of my decision whether or not to leave my marriage, I was ready to investigate that aspect of my life: My own orgasm—a part of myself that had been, as of yet, dormant and unlived.

I wanted to feel sensation, I told them. For so long, I'd turned off my feelings because the bad ones had been so painful. But that caused me to go numb so that I couldn't experience orgasm or other good feelings. I wanted to be turned on, and I thought OM might help.

I had no idea.

Up until this point, my life had been more discipline than celebration. I had been into self-inflicted restraint since I was young. I'd been bulimic in my late teens and early twenties; I'd loved the feeling of strategically regulating every morsel I ate, and then the relief I felt upon elimination.

Looking back, I see it was my fear of chaos that had me attempting to control anything I believed I *could* control, most significantly, my own body. I became very skilled at compartmentalizing my feelings and cutting myself off from my emotions. I'd grown up believing I was too heavy, and bulimia provided a way to manage my anxiety around that. This was right at the height of the exercise craze of the 80s. I remember practically wearing out my Jane Fonda record (yes, record!), as I diligently scissor-kicked my way through her workout several times a day.

Finally, a roommate of mine called my parents to let them know the secret I'd been keeping. They found a therapist for me, and I learned to look for the underlying cause behind the outward manifestation of my eating disorder.

It wasn't until I was twenty-five that I first experienced loving and accepting my body. And it happened in a pretty unconventional way.

It was my twenty-fifth birthday, and I was lying on a nude beach in Greece. I had a fleeting thought—"I wonder if there's a way to make money doing this?"

When I got back to New York City, I joked about it to a friend who told me that the School of Visual Arts was always looking for nude models. Wow. Modeling? *Nude* modeling? For *artists*? "Sign me up!" I thought. I went on to model full time for two years, and continued off and on for several years after that.

Being studied, drawn, painted, photographed, and sculpted somehow got me into right relationship with my body. I saw myself over and over again, from the perspective of others. I saw myself sometimes admired, sometimes distorted, but always revered.

Ironically, working as a nude model catalyzed my pursuit of a master's degree—in Poetry. I was trying to decide between an MFA and an MBA. Spending so much time around art students who were pursuing their passions and not worrying about money, I was inspired to follow my heart, too. It led me all the way to Naropa University in Boulder, Colorado.

I thought I would get my master's degree and then go back to New York City to teach, but life had other plans. I had met the man I would marry, and his outdoorsy lifestyle had heavily influenced me. After my two-year program was finished, I stayed.

Throughout my thirties and early forties I was once again obsessed with my body. No more bulimia, thank goodness, but for years I over-exercised and went through periods of extreme dietary restriction. I wouldn't go near sugar, especially chocolate. I prided myself on the "success"—low body-fat, muscle definition, self-control—that my deprivation awarded me. What I didn't realize, until I came out from under its spell, was the toll this obsession had taken on me. My adrenals were shot. My sense of joy was depleted. My desire for pleasure was MIA. I can't remember feeling much of anything except for the compulsive drive to work and maintain my body.

Enter OM.

Toward the end of my session with the OM coaches, they invited a man and a woman into the room to demonstrate the OM practice for me. As you can imagine, I was slightly uncomfortable! I had never witnessed anything of the sort, especially not so up close and personal. But as I watched, I saw the woman come to life under his steady gaze. It was as if his unwavering attention wed her desire, and the two became one.

For me, it was also like that deli scene in the movie *When Harry Met Sally* when Meg Ryan demonstrates faking an orgasm. Another patron says, "I'll have what she's having!"

The coaches asked if I'd like to set up an OM for some time over the next couple of days. I told them I was ready right then and there. I didn't want another minute to go by before that place in me could be unconcealed and accessed.

Enter the "master stroker" – and my first OM.

My whole conception of who I was changed in that fifteen minutes. Having repressed my hunger for so long, I was shocked at the eruption that was unearthed within me. It was beyond any chaos I could have imagined. Sensation infused me with a life force I had never known.

Kelly was waiting for me outside. As we walked to a nearby restaurant for lunch, it was as if everything had changed. All of my senses were heightened. Walking down the street—the same one I'd walked down an hour earlier—I felt like Dorothy landing in a Technicolor Oz. We went to a tiny trattoria and sat out on the patio. All the sights, sounds, smells, and tastes mingled in the sunshine. A handsome young waiter brought our meals. I don't really even know if he was that handsome, but I was firing on all cylinders, and he sure *felt* handsome to me! Or maybe it was just that he was delivering bowls of decadent homemade pasta to our table—pasta unlike anything I'd ever tasted. I asked myself when the last time was—if ever—that I had allowed myself to actually enjoy food (or anything) this much. It didn't matter; as far as I was concerned, that lunch was the best lunch I had ever eaten. After a lifetime of restriction, I willingly surrendered and savored. Food had never been so inviting, delectable, or satisfying.

I had been starving to death before OM awakened me to my own hunger and desire.

At the end of the meal, Kelly asked if I wanted to walk across the street to buy a piece of her favorite chocolate. "Sure," I said, nonchalantly, as if I bought chocolate every day of the week.

In truth, it had been months since I'd had chocolate in my mouth, months since I felt the warm, oozy richness melt across my tongue. It isn't that I didn't love chocolate; it was that I, Nancy Levin, did not eat it. It was a point of pride. Others might be weak enough to indulge themselves, but that was a choice for them to make. Not me. I was a black belt at resisting temptation. Every time an indulgence was offered and I refused, I got a little gold star in my own internal rating system.

That day in San Francisco, I think I consciously intended to walk with Kelly and keep her company while she bought the chocolate. I'd already indulged so much! The OM, the pasta, even flirting with the waiter! But something else was emerging within me— something beyond my volition. An irrevocable internal shift had begun. As if watching myself from some point outside of my own being, I saw my hand reach out and pick up the same bar of chocolate Kelly was getting.

"I'm buying," she said, taking it out of my hand and moving toward the cashier. I walked behind her, somewhat stunned at what was happening. I was vaguely aware she was still chatting with me about something or other, but I was barely listening.

Luckily, Kelly had to run off to a meeting as soon as we emerged from the store. Knowing she was saving her chocolate for later was a great relief to me because it meant I didn't have to make the decision about eating it or not in that moment. Maybe just buying it was enough.

Maybe living the rest of my life without joy and pleasure was enough. Maybe living the rest of my life without rich, yummy, nurturing, crazy, wild, and free sex was enough. Maybe living the rest of my life clinging to my gold stars of deprivation was enough. Maybe living the rest of my life without living at all was enough. But of course, none of that was enough.

I took the Muni train back to my sister's house, and that evening, all alone, after much internal negotiation, I gave myself permission to take a bite. I said yes to just one. The chocolate snapped decadently against my teeth. Soon, its warmth was unpacking itself against the roof of my mouth, and as it softened and melted across my tongue—dark, rustic, buttery—I swear, deep down inside, I felt some barrier around my heart melt as well. The automatic "N" and "O" dissolved, and I swallowed the no without bitterness, instead saying, "Yes, yes, yes!"

Make Yes a Habit

You can bet that the old me would have said no to that OM experience, let alone the chocolate. But what I discovered is that saying yes to what you desire or what intrigues you is a profound act of self-love.

So, allow your desires to draw you toward joy, and invite the divine to bring you more new opportunities. Invite the unscripted, the unexpected. Do that one different thing. Practice by saying yes to something you might ordinarily say no to out of habit. Maybe you're like me, and your habit has been to say no to things that you deemed impractical (like vacations—for years, I thought they were frivolous). Let go of that habit—just once to start. Test it out. Yes, you're ready. You can do it.

The opportunities that come your way are your gifts. That doesn't mean you have to jump on every bandwagon that rolls by, but set aside your fears long enough to imagine what good could come from saying yes. Avoid saying no to something just because you're afraid, because you worry what others might think, or because you think it's "different," "weird," or "strange." (Different, weird, and strange can be fascinating! Remember my OM story.) Recognize, too, that sometimes saying yes to what you want will mean saying no to someone else. (If that's difficult for you, review step five, Set Your New Boundaries.)

Heather Tells Her Story

In my early thirties, I was a successful executive who was burning a path up the corporate ladder. I had worked in a handful of industries and did very well. As a "get-it done" people-pleaser, I was convinced that working really hard was the key to my success. And apparently I was in good company, because I had joined a firm well known in the industry for burning out their type A employees.

A few years after joining the firm, I began to look at my colleagues and listen to their stories. What astounded me was that no one above the director level in the company was truly healthy. One of the executives collapsed in the stairwell. Another had to have major stomach surgery for stress-related

---

autoimmune illness. Many others had migraines, chronic fatigue, and a whole host of issues that kept them feeling less than well, but still allowed them to show up at work and do their jobs.

Admittedly, I was facing my own health challenges and realized that I did not want to join their ranks. I began to understand the emptiness of having it all on the surface, but feeling neither happy, nor healthy, behind the scenes. As my health suffered, I knew that in order to turn the ship around, I had to decide that my health and well-being were more important than my job.

It was a major dilemma. Should I leave my job? What would I do? I was at one of those "golden handcuffs" companies where they pay you more and more the longer you stay. The perks and extras sat in front of me like a carrot that could virtually guarantee financial independence if I only stayed five or ten more years. On top of that, I was not a "quitter." I felt a lot of shame just thinking of quitting when I was so close to the brass ring and had no other great job lined up.

And I was scared. I was the major breadwinner for my family, so how would we pay the bills? After fifteen years in the corporate world, would I be able to survive or even make any money if I went out on my own?

I had no answers to these questions. What I did have was this tiny whisper in the back of my mind telling me to take the leap. It literally felt like I was making the decision to jump off a cliff. I would see myself looking over the edge, and I kept wondering if there would be a net to catch me. The whisper in the back of my mind kept saying, "If you don't jump, how will you ever know?"

That was the key for me. I could stay locked in a room with the devil I knew or jump off that cliff and see if I could fly on my own. I decided to jump. For a period of time after giving my notice at work, the shame I felt about "quitting" was transformed into wonder. Each day, several colleagues would come into my office and tell me about their big dreams. Since I was leaving to pursue my dreams with no big, fancy job lined up, they felt safe telling me about theirs. In this big, conservative corporation, I had colleagues with dreams not so far off from my own. They wanted a simpler life, work they were passionate about, and to get off the hamster wheel.

They were more spiritual than they had let on. They were excited for me and even a bit envious. They were just as scared about the money, just as scared to take a leap.

Over the next nine years, I coached high performers in business and saw many miracles as they pursued their dreams. And you know what? Each one of them got healthier as they made choices to honor what was in their hearts.

Within three months of leaving my job, I knew that no matter what they paid me, I'd never go back. And today, I am grateful for taking that leap. I learned to trust life, to trust I was safe financially ... and most of all, to trust that tiny whisper in the back of my mind.

Jumping as a Way of Life

As you make your jump and learn to say yes more often, here's an important truth to keep in mind: There is no destination. You're never "there." You're always becoming. You'll always be jumping—over and over and over. And that's a good thing.

When so many new opportunities came my way after leaving my marriage, I thought to myself, "I must remember that it happens this way! If I let go, trust, and jump, I will be safe and showered with extraordinary surprises." Even though the change was very painful at times, I didn't die the first time I jumped, and I could remind myself I wouldn't die the next time either!

At some point after your decision to leap into your new life, the foundation might begin to crack beneath you and crumble again. You will probably find yourself at the edge of an all-too-familiar cliff, terrified to jump, and struggling to remember that you were safe with ground growing below you, supporting your courage and willingness to change. When that happens, remind yourself of what happened when you jumped before. Allow the wiser part of you to counsel the frightened part of you. Even if the transition was difficult, recall the many rewards that awaited you on the other side.

Regular small jumps followed by big leaps are a part of the package. In order to risk anything, we have to be willing to risk everything.

Of course, I realize that releasing your fears about jumping into the unknown is easier said than done. We want to know we're jumping *to* something else. We want an ironclad guarantee that the new thing will be better than what we're leaving. But without a time machine, we can never be absolutely sure the next moment is going to be better than the last.

The goal is not to arrive at a destination but to get to the point where your whole life is one big leap. Life is like a video game—the reward for winning one level is an even harder level. You simply become more comfortable with spontaneity and with the invitation to change.

Buddhist nun Pema Chödrön put it this way: "We think that the point is to pass the test or overcome the problem, but the truth is that things don't really get solved. They come together, and they fall apart. Then, they come together again and fall apart again. It's just like that. The healing comes from letting there be room for all of this to happen; room for grief, for relief, for misery, for joy."

So, you begin to look for the jumps, for what is waiting for you, for what you can change, for what you can say yes to. Ironically, you begin to feel comfortable outside of your comfort zone, and you welcome the feeling of being slightly off balance because you enjoy the growth process.

I recently reached a more advanced level in mountain biking. What happened next? I crashed. I got a bit bruised, but I got right back up on the bike and went for another ride the next day, looking again for routes that would cause me to come up with a new strategy and sharpen my skills.

Let changing your life become a *way* of life. The word for courage comes from "coeur," the French word for heart. Open your heart to possibility, and you will find courage you didn't even know you had.

Letting go of fear and surrendering to love has allowed me to soften my grip on the way I *thought* my life *should* be. In the cradle of that love, my life as it actually *is* has emerged. And it's very good.

My coaching client Tracy put it this way: "My yes today is about yes to whatever, whoever I am right at this moment. Radical acceptance! I haven't let go of fear; I have befriended it. I haven't learned to move faster, but slower, with more care and attention to how I'm *really* feeling. To be responsible is to be response-able, and I now understand I need a certain kind of rhythm, slow-paced, to be able to listen to my internal intuition and to respond. I have planted a garden in my soul, and I tend to it. To move from a place of love and excitement, I need to be deeply rooted in this garden and intimately conversing with my heart. The rest is all taken care of. All is always well when I'm my best ally."

As Fritz Perls, founder of Gestalt therapy, has said, "Fear is excitement without the breath." So, breathe!

Say Yes to Love and No to Fear

1. What would happen if you let love, excitement, and passion move you—instead of fear? What would you do if you were totally free, without fear? Imagine that you are someone without any fear of following your heart, and live your life as that person for twenty-four hours. What would you do differently? How would your life look compared to the way it looks now?

2. Fill in the blanks all five times. Here's an example: "I used to be afraid of having fun, and now I seek out chances to have fun and experience joy."

I used to _____, and now I ___
_____

I used to _____, and now
I _____

I used to_____, and now I ___
_____

I used to_____, and now I ___
_____

I used to_____, and now I ___
_____

3. Write down five to ten things you will say yes to in the next month:

I will say yes to _____
I will say yes to _____
I will say yes to _____
I will say yes to _____
I will say yes to _____
I will say yes to _____
I will say yes to _____
I will say yes to _____
I will say yes to _____
I will say yes to _____

A MOMENT TO LOVE

Instead of A MOMENT TO FORGIVE at the end of this step, I want to invite you to love yourself more. Through loving yourself, your capacity to love others actually increases. How do you love yourself more? Simply think of someone you love with all your heart, and imagine what it would be like to turn that love back toward yourself. Can you do it? If not, practice until you can take all of that love into your heart. You deserve it. I mean it. Remember: You don't have to be perfect. No one is—not even that person you love so dearly, even if that person is a child.

Open your heart to the belief that you deserve. Open your ability to receive. Increase your "having-ness" level. Begin to imagine what it would be like to receive more. Notice your resistance. Give love to any parts of you that feel you don't deserve. Why not you? Allow yourself to receive a little bit … and a little bit more … continuing to build on your ability to accept wonderful things into your life.

I hope that this process will help you dance into the life that you deserve.

The last words that my dear friend, the late Debbie Ford, ever said to me were: "Go live your life. Don't work yourself to death. I love you, babydoll."

So, I echo her words: *Go live your life—the one you were meant to live.*

Nancy Levin

unbound

we may never know
how we hold
all we can
or how the light catches us
when we are out of breath

it's a sign of healing
to be feeling again

the real breakthrough
can only arise
from heartbreak

that which ails
cures
reminding us
that it's always about beginning
and then beginning again

as the waves crash me
i trust the sand
to polish my edges smooth
dissolving denial
revealing real
while courage and confidence
ignite my core

contraction and expansion
let the light stream in
and the stillness
after so much thrashing about
allows the body to wring
the sorrow out

as freedom floods
shadows may persist
know your undertow
as you alchemize the dark
and remember
that you always have
the strength to choose
how to engage

the clouds unveil the view
when you are ready to climb
now it's time to notice
the miraculous moments
in your life
as they are happening

this
is the making
of me
and we will walk
courageously
into daybreak
from the night
shining our light
together

Acknowledgments

As a testament to what I learned as a result of Step 6, I asked for help – and a lot of it! I couldn't have made it through my process alone, and this book wouldn't be in your hands right now without the extraordinary help of some exceptional people.

"Thank you" doesn't begin to embody what my soul wants to express. I am beyond grateful to everyone here for their love and support.

Louise Hay: For being my "personalized affirmation action figure!" What an honor to accompany you on your journey in this lifetime.

Reid Tracy: For being my biggest cheerleader and for believing in me long before I did.

Cheryl Richardson: For truly teaching me what it is to hold someone else in her highest and for providing safety, faith, and all those mornings in the round room.

Debbie Ford: What I wouldn't give to curl up in bed with you one more time. It is with great honor and grace that I carry your legacy forward.

Melanie Votaw: For weaving your magical elegance with my voice and words.

All the people who shared their stories: For your transparency, and wholehearted commitment to truth and change.

Michelle Polizzi: For being a joy to work with on this cover design.

Richard Cummings: For making my first-ever photo shoot so fun and fruitful.

Sandy Powell and Jennifer Slaybaugh at Balboa Press: For your enthusiasm and patience with my publishing process.

Margarete Nielsen: For seeing in me what I couldn't, and for having my back while helping me hold the vision.

Maya Labos: For being my other mother.

Mollie Langer, Jen Simmons, Matt Wood, Donna Abate, Andrea Kraus, Brian Mitrisin and Amy Kazor: For being my phenomenal team behind the scenes. I appreciate each of you so much.

Julie Stroud (aka "Saint Julie"), Kelley Kosow, Fran Fusco, The Ford Institute and my fellow coaches: For being family.

Kris Carr and Kate Northrup: For our conversation sitting on the floor in Ink 48's lobby bar encouraging me to share my truth. Deep gratitude.

Nick Ortner: For your unparalleled moral support and of course tapping, especially backstage, for better or worse.

Maria Bailey, Gabrielle Bernstein, Joan Borysenko, Gregg Braden, Anastacia Brice, Barbara Carrellas, Teri Cole, Heather Dane, Wayne Dyer, Arielle Ford, Sarah Grace, Brian Hilliard, Ibis Kaba, Ahlea Khadro, Elizabeth Lesser, Denise Linn, Kate Mackinnon, Karen McCrocklin, Caroline Myss, Christiane Northrup, Daniel Peralta, Linda Perry, Wendy Perkins, Susan Tzankow, Doreen Virtue, Meggan Watterson, Marianne Williamson, Alex Woodard, Richelle Zizian: With much love for the singular role that each of you plays along the way.

Patty Gift: For your expansive heart and soul companionship as we roam about.

Kelly Notaras: For your fierce grace, dedication and devotion to me and to this project. But mostly just for being the other half of us.

Aaron Thomas: For your heartfelt willingness and desire to learn, grow, teach, share, play and love with me.

Mom and Dad: For everything. Really.

Kate: For being the other half of my heartbeat...and for sharing Allan, Isabel and Simon with me.

About the Author

Nancy Levin is a Certified Integrative Coach through The Ford Institute For Transformational Training and the author of *Writing For My Life*. Since 2002, she's been the Event Director at Hay House, producing experiential events and innovative conferences, focusing on self-empowerment, health and spirituality, while weaving in her own story and poems to connect with audiences around the world during keynotes, workshops and seminars. When she's not on an airplane, Nancy lives in Boulder, Colorado where she received her MFA in Poetics from Naropa University. You can visit her online at www.nancylevin.com

Need Support While Jumping?

*Schedule your **complimentary**
jump-start session with me today.*

I will coach you – inch-by-inch – through
the process of your major change.

Receive firsthand experience of what would be available
to you if we were to engage in a coaching partnership.

Let me support you
in taking powerful,
consistent, accountable
action each week.

I am here to ensure
that you create deep
and lasting change.

*Visit **nancylevin.com**
to take your first step in
moving from where you are
– to where you want to be.*

Due to the nature of this work, I only
coach a handful of clients at a time.
Reserve your place in my practice, today!

Click … And Your Coach Will Appear!

nancylevin.com